ALTA VIA 1 – TREKKING IN THE DOLOMITES

INCLUDES 1:25,000 MAP BOOKLET

ALTA VIA 1 – TREKKING IN THE DOLOMITES

INCLUDES 1:25,000 MAP BOOKLET

by Gillian Price

JUNIPER HOUSE, MURLEY MOSS,
OXENHOLME ROAD, KENDAL, CUMBRIA LA9 7RL
www.cicerone.co.uk

© Gillian Price 2022
Fifth edition 2022
ISBN: 978 1 78631 081 1
Reprinted 2023 (with updates)
Fourth edition 2016
Third edition 2011
Second edition 2005
First edition 1990

Printed in China on responsibly sourced paper on behalf of Latitude Press Ltd
A catalogue record for this book is available from the British Library.

Route mapping by Lovell Johns www.lovelljohns.com

Contains OpenStreetMap.org data © OpenStreetMap contributors, CC-BY-SA.
NASA relief data courtesy of ESRI

Mapping in map booklet © KOMPASSKarten GmbH
cartography 2022 (licence number: 41-0921-LIV).
Copying and reproduction prohibited

All photographs are by the author unless otherwise stated.

For the one-and-only Nick, companion and joke-teller supreme.

Acknowledgements

Thanks to all the walkers who wrote in with helpful feedback and comments
on previous editions.

Front cover: Alta Via 1 passes through Forcella Travenanzes on Stage 4

CONTENTS

Updates to this Guide

While every effort is made by our authors to ensure the accuracy of guide-books as they go to print, changes can occur during the lifetime of an edition. Any updates that we know of for this guide will be on the Cicerone website (www.cicerone.co.uk/1081/updates), so please check before planning your trip. We also advise that you check information about such things as transport, accommodation and shops locally. Even rights of way can be altered over time.

We are always grateful for information about any discrepancies between a guidebook and the facts on the ground, sent by email to updates@cicerone.co.uk or by post to Cicerone, Juniper House, Murley Moss, Oxenholme Road, Kendal, LA9 7RL.

Register your book: To sign up to receive free updates, special offers and GPX files where available, register your book at www.cicerone.co.uk.

Note on mapping

The route maps in this guide are derived from publicly available data, data-bases and crowd-sourced data. As such they have not been through the detailed checking procedures that would generally be applied to a published map from an official mapping agency. However, we have reviewed them closely in the light of local knowledge as part of the preparation of this guide.

Symbols used on route maps

~	route
- - -	alternative route
Ⓢ	start point
Ⓕ	finish point
>	route direction
	woodland
	urban areas
•	other feature
🚠	cable car
🚡	chair lift
▲	peak
🔺	mountain hut
◌	other accommodation
🍴	food
◼	bus stop/station
P	parking
†	cross
⤨	pass
🛈	tourist information
=	footbridge

Relief
in metres

3600–3800
3400–3600
3200–3400
3000–3200
2800–3000
2600–2800
2400–2600
2200–2400
2000–2200
1800–2000
1600–1800
1400–1600
1200–1400
1000–1200
800–1000
600–800
400–600
200–400
0–200

SCALE: 1:75,000

0   0.5   1 kms

0   0.5 miles

Contour lines are drawn at 25m intervals and highlighted at 100m intervals.

GPX files for all routes can be downloaded free at www.cicerone.co.uk/1081/GPX.

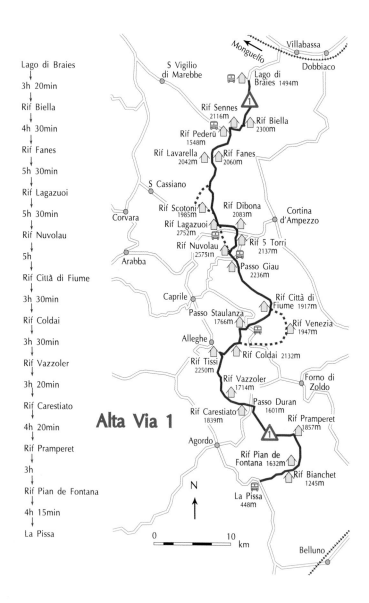

Lago di Braies
↓ 3h 20min
Rif Biella
↓ 4h 30min
Rif Fanes
↓ 5h 30min
Rif Lagazuoi
↓ 5h 30min
Rif Nuvolau
↓ 5h
Rif Città di Fiume
↓ 3h 30min
Rif Coldai
↓ 3h 30min
Rif Vazzoler
↓ 3h 20min
Rif Carestiato
↓ 4h 20min
Rif Pramperet
↓ 3h
Rif Pian de Fontana
↓ 4h 15min
La Pissa

Villabassa
Monguelfo
Dobbiaco
S Vigilio di Marebbe
Lago di Braies 1494m
Rif Sennes 2116m
Rif Biella 2300m
Rif Pederü 1548m
Rif Lavarella 2042m
Rif Fanes 2060m
S Cassiano
Rif Scotoni 1985m
Rif Dibona 2083m
Cortina d'Ampezzo
Corvara
Rif Lagazuoi 2752m
Rif Nuvolau 2575m
Rif 5 Torri 2137m
Arabba
Passo Giau 2236m
Caprile
Rif Città di Fiume 1917m
Passo Staulanza 1766m
Rif Venezia 1947m
Alleghe
Rif Coldai 2132m
Rif Tissi 2250m
Rif Vazzoler 1714m
Forno di Zoldo
Passo Duran 1601m
Rif Carestiato 1839m
Rif Pramperet 1857m

Alta Via 1

Agordo
Rif Pian de Fontana 1632m
Rif Bianchet 1245m
La Pissa 448m
N
0   10 km
Belluno

ROUTE SUMMARY TABLE

Stage	From	To	Time	Distance	Ascent	Descent	Grade	Page
1	Lago di Braies	Rifugio Biella	3hr 20min	6km	870m	60m	2	37
2	Rifugio Biella	Rifugio Fanes	4hr 30min	13km	710m	980m	1	42
3	Rifugio Fanes	Rifugio Lagazuoi	5hr 30min	12.2km	1150m	450m	2	48
4	Rifugio Lagazuoi	Rifugio Nuvolau	5hr 30min	12.8km	1100m	1275m	2	54
5	Rifugio Nuvolau	Rifugio Città di Fiume	5hr	12.8km	500m	1200m	2–3	63
6	Rifugio Città di Fiume	Rifugio Coldai	3hr 30min	9.3km	560m	340m	2	69
7	Rifugio Coldai	Rifugio Vazzoler	3hr 30min	9.8km	450m	850m	2	77
8	Rifugio Vazzoler	Rifugio Carestiato	3hr 20min	8.7km	620m	500m	2+	82
9	Rifugio Carestiato	Rifugio Pramperet	4hr 20min	13.2km	620m	600m	2	86
10	Rifugio Pramperet	Rifugio Pian de Fontana	3hr	6.2km	540m	760m	2–3	91
11	Rifugio Pian de Fontana	La Pissa bus stop	4hr 15min	11km	200m	1400m	2	95
Total	Lago di Braies	La Pissa bus stop	45hr 45min	115km	7320m	8415m		

Mountain safety

Every mountain walk has its dangers, and those described in this guidebook are no exception. All who walk or climb in the mountains should recognise this and take responsibility for themselves and their companions along the way. The author and publisher have made every effort to ensure that the information contained in this guide was correct when it went to press, but, except for any liability that cannot be excluded by law, they cannot accept responsibility for any loss, injury or inconvenience sustained by any person using this book.

International distress signal *(emergency only)*
Six blasts on a whistle (and flashes with a torch after dark) spaced evenly for one minute, followed by a minute's pause. Repeat until an answer is received. The response is three signals per minute followed by a minute's pause.

Helicopter rescue
The following signals are used to communicate with a helicopter:

Help needed:
raise both arms
above head to
form a 'Y'

Help not needed:
raise one arm
above head, extend
other arm downward

Emergency telephone numbers
If telephoning from overseas the dialling code for *Italy* is +39

General emergency tel 112
Soccorso alpino (mountain rescue) tel 118

Weather reports
Südtirol https://weather.provinz.bz.it
Trentino www.meteotrentino.it
Veneto www.arpa.veneto.it

Mountain rescue can be very expensive – be adequately insured.

PREFACE TO THIS EDITION

I'm thrilled to be presenting this new edition of the magnificent Alta Via 1. The Dolomites are by far my favourite mountains, and this is easily one of my favourite long-distance treks. My very first AV1 was back in 1981, an experience both awe-inspiring and unforgettable – not least because Nicola and I braved a storm and lashing rain equipped with little but bin liners as rainskirts. I've since lost count of trek repeats, but I can say for sure that levels of excitement and satisfaction increase on each occasion, not to mention comfort in the huts.

This brand new edition provides up-to-date details that will help make this beautiful trek even easier to handle and organise, and it is supplemented with new mapping in a separate booklet.

UNESCO added the Dolomites to its World Heritage list in 2009 and visitor numbers have soared. Now it is even more important to emphasise more responsible management helped by environment-conscious walkers to ensure this paradise can be enjoyed by future generations.

Gillian Price, Venice

The paths coasts below Becco di Mezzodì (Stage 15)

Rifugio Fanes backed by Sasso della Croce (Stage 2)

INTRODUCTION

Rifugio Biella is only a short descent from Forcella Sora Forno (Stage 1)

THE DOLOMITES

What can visitors to the Dolomites expect? This description from travel writer John Murray in 1840 helps set the stage:

They are unlike any other mountains, and are to be seen nowhere else among the Alps. They arrest the attention by the singularity and picturesqueness of their forms, by their sharp peaks or horns, sometimes rising up in pinnacles and obelisks, at others extending in serrated ridges, teethed like the jaw of an alligator.

Tucked up in the northeastern corner of Italy close to the border with Austria, the Dolomite mountains embrace an extraordinary array of spectacular landscapes – a wonderland for outdoor enthusiasts. Rather than a continuous alpine chain, these are unique self-contained rock formations, instantly recognisable: the soaring pyramidal Tofane, the Sella fortress, throne-shaped Pelmo and the incredible sheer-faced Civetta are just a few of the giants that become trail companions for trekkers. Their peaks rise to dizzy heights, sculpted with delicately pale rock spires and

The Pelmo over Passo Staulanza (Stage 6)

breathtaking walls towering over lunar-like plateaux where people are hardly dots. Clocking in at 3342m is the majestic Marmolada ('Queen of the Dolomites'), the highest of them all, clutching its rapidly shrinking glacier. Well below are dense evergreen and deciduous forests, home to fascinating wildlife, and alpine meadows transformed into veritable seas of wildflowers in summer. Pure delight for nature lovers.

Beautiful valleys with picturesque, hospitable villages and facilities to suit all budgets are linked by good roads and excellent public transport. And a superb web of marked pathways snake over mountain and vale, conveniently punctuated with *rifugi* mountain huts and comfortable guesthouses that welcome walkers, feed them royally and give them a bed for the night.

THE ROUTE

What better way to explore these incredible mountains than on a long-distance trek? Beginners need go no further than the popular high-level trail Alta Via 1 (abbreviated as AV1) – straightforward yet astoundingly rewarding, and perfectly suited for a first alpine experience. Well way-marked and easy to follow on well-trodden paths, it is spread over 11 days and covers 115km, reaching a high point of 2752m. An estimated 80% of all the Dolomites can be seen from the AV1 as it threads its way through the Fanes group then over the Lagazuoi, touching on the Tofane, Averau and Nuvolau, the landmark Pelmo, Civetta, Moiazza and the rugged Dolomiti Bellunesi. (The handy 'PeakFinder' app will help you put all the right names to the mountains you see.)

During World War 1, as conflict raged between the crumbling Austro-Hungarian Empire and fledgling Italy, the Dolomites became a tragic war zone, with contested borders running along high-altitude mountain ridges and mule tracks snaking up valleys. Common along the AV1, ruins of barracks, trenches and rusting barbed wire are chilling reminders of the madness of war.

OTHER ALTA VIA ROUTES

Six established Alta Via walking trails traverse the Dolomites from top to bottom, north to south, maintaining medium to high altitude and exploring spectacular corners of different groups – such as the Puez-Odle to Sella, Marmolada to the Pale di San Martino, Sesto to the Marmarole. Of a more demanding flavour than AV1, the remaining five can be found in the separate guidebook *Alta Via 2 – Trekking in the Dolomites with AV3–6*.

The trek makes overnight stops at manned mountain huts, so on the whole you can travel light. Naturally, self-sufficient trekkers can camp out, enabling great flexibility and freedom, although restrictions do apply – see 'Accommodation'.

In this guide the route is described in the classic north–south direction, but it can easily be walked south–north by recalculating times in relation to ascent/descent. Moreover, at a handful of places along the way, detours are possible to villages with shops and other facilities. Such exit routes are essential in emergencies, bad weather or a change of plan; they also make handy alternative ways to access the AV1 if you prefer to customise the trek to fit in with personal holiday dictates. All exit routes are explained clearly at the appropriate spot in the route description, along with transport options.

GEOLOGY

A little geology goes a long way in understanding the Dolomites. The Monti Pallidi or 'Pale Mounts', as they were originally called, were rechristened in honour of a French mineralogist marquis with the unforgettable name Déodat Guy Sylvain Tancrède Gratet de Dolomieu. On a 1789 visit he identified the main rock as calcium magnesium carbonate (later known as dolomite), which shares the show with limestone, namely calcium carbonate.

The mountains date back some 230 million years to when the region was covered by a shallow tropical sea. Remains of sea creatures, coral and much else accumulated on its floor. These compressed and hardened over time into sedimentary rock which incorporates fossilised shells, ripple marks and even intriguing dinosaur tracks. Much later, around 65 million years ago, land-moving tectonic events thrust the rock dramatically upwards, as the Alps were created. Over time, ice ages and glaciers shaped the mountains, and they are subject to ongoing erosion by wind and rain – the vast scree flows are a good example.

At sundown the pale rock faces of the Dolomites assume gorgeous hues of orangey-pink, a spectacular phenomenon known by the Ladin term *enrosadira*.

PLANTS AND FLOWERS

The Dolomites boast 1400 species of flowering plants – around a fifth of Italy's total. Throughout the summer months it's impossible not to be impressed by the incredible spreads of blooms in the most unlikely and inhospitable spots. Heading the list in popularity, thanks to its appearance in *The Sound of Music*, is the edelweiss. While not spectacular, it has creamy felty petals in a star formation and grows either prostrate or upright on stony terrain. The flower is said to

have been brought from the moon for a legendary princess – a memento of the pale lunar landscape to which she was accustomed.

In dramatic colour contrast are the deep-blue trumpet gentians that burst through the grass, demanding admiration. In lush meadows, orange lilies and the wine-red martagon variety vie with each other for brilliance. Light larch woodland and slopes are colonised by spreads of alpenrose – a type of rhododendron that has masses of pretty red-pink flowers. Its neighbours are low bushes of bilberries,

(Clockwise from top L) Orange lily; Rhaetian poppies; king of the Alps; Moretti's bellflower

laden with tiny sweet fruit in late summer.

One of the earliest blooms to appear is the Alpine snowbell; its fragile fringed blue-lilac bells even sprout in snow patches, thanks to an 'antifreeze' carbohydrate. Never far away are delicate pasque flowers in white or yellow.

Shaded clearings are the place to look for the unusual lady's-slipper orchid, recognisable by a swollen yellow lip crowned by maroon petals, while pyramidal purple or cone-shaped black vanilla orchids are common on rich pasture. Perfumed fluttery Rhaetian poppies brighten bleached scree slopes with patches of yellow and orange, companions to clumps of pink thrift or round-leaved pennycress, which is honey-scented. Another rock coloniser is saxifrage, literally 'rock breaker', so called for its deep-reaching roots.

A rare treat is devil's claw, which specialises in hanging off vertical rock faces. A member of the rampion family, it sports a segmented pointy lilac flower with curly stigma. Another precious bloom is the king of the Alps, a striking cushion of pretty blue, almost a dwarf version of the forget-me-not. Moretti's bellflower, with blue-purple petals, nestles in high crevices in the southern Dolomites. Dry sun-scorched terrain is preferred by curious houseleeks, which bear an uncanny resemblance to miniature triffids.

As for trees, over 1000m is the realm of conifers such as silver fir along with 'high achievers' arolla pine and larch, which can reach altitudes of 2600m. A great coloniser and anchor on scree is the dwarf mountain pine, whose springy branches invade paths. One remarkable 'bonsai' tree is the net-leaved willow, whose closely packed root system creeps over rock surfaces.

WILDLIFE

It seems a miracle that wild animals still call the European Alps home. As if the harsh environment and climate weren't enough, they also have to deal with ongoing threats from mankind in the shape of roads, expanding ski pistes and resorts; selective hunting is also allowed in some valleys, albeit under strict controls. The good news is that much of the Dolomites comes under the protection of nature parks: Dolomiti di Sesto, Sciliar, Puez-Odle, Pale di San Martino, Fanes-Senes-Braies, Dolomiti d'Ampezzo and Dolomiti Bellunesi – and the AV1 traverses the latter three.

The animals you're most likely to see when out walking are alpine marmots. These adorable furry creatures look a bit like beavers (without the flat tail) and live in extensive underground colonies. Wary of foxes and golden eagles who can carry off their young, they always have a sentry posted – an older animal that stands rod-straight and emits heart-stopping warning whistles to summon the tribe back home. Alpine marmots hibernate

Alpine marmot

Chamois

from October to April, waking once a month to urinate. Now protected in Italy, they were once hunted for their skins and fat, and paraded in street fairs.

Higher up, impossibly steep rock faces and scree slopes are the ideal terrain for shy, fleet-hoofed chamois – slender mountain goats with short crochet-hook horns and fawn coats. Herds of females with their young graze on pasture flats, separate from old itinerant males whose sharp poignant whistle gives them away in the bushes. Chamois head down into valleys when the snow starts falling, sharing the forest habitat with graceful Bambi-like roe deer and the rarer large red species.

Ibex are an exciting sight. These stocky animals sport impressively thick grooved horns that curve backwards, up to a metre long on males, who can weigh 100kg; the females less on both counts. During the summer, young males spend time in mock battle clashing their horns in preparation for the December mating season when it is anything but pretend, as the females are only on heat for 24 hours. Ibex were successfully re-introduced to the Dolomites in the 1970s from the single surviving group in the whole of the Alps – the Gran Paradiso National Park in the Valle d'Aosta.

Brown bears once roamed the Dolomites, as testified by place names such as Col dell'Orso (bear's col) and Buco dell'Orso (bear's hole). They were hunted to near extinction in the 1800s, but a tiny nucleus hung on in the western Dolomites. Now protected, their numbers have been boosted by arrivals from Slovenia; the population is currently estimated at 50–60. Sightings and fleeting encounters are becoming more common in the Trentino region, where they are an increasing nuisance to both shepherds and beekeepers.

The European wolf, on the other hand, has required no help at all. Originating from a group in the central Apennines, over recent years elegant grey wolves have come north and spread stealthily all across the Italian Alps, successfully establishing packs and sometimes attacking livestock when wild prey is unavailable. In the extremely unlikely event that you see either of these animals, use your common sense and keep your distance. Under no circumstances should they be approached.

Now that terrible dragons have been banished from the Alps, the only other potentially dangerous encounters concern snakes and ticks. Hot weather and open terrain could mean an encounter with an adder or viper (*vipera* in Italian). Tawny brown with a diamond-shaped head and distinctive zigzag markings along its back, they grow up to 70cm. Vipers are venomous but only attack under threat, so if you meet one – on a path where it's sunning itself and may be sluggish – step back and give it time to slither away to safety. In the unlikely event of a bite (very rarely fatal), stay put and seek help immediately.

As regards the tick – *zecca* in Italian – some may carry Lyme disease or TBE (tick-borne encephalitis), life-threatening for humans. Warnings apply for the southern Dolomites (crossed during the closing days of AV1), especially wooded areas with thick undergrowth where ticks can latch onto you. Precautions include wearing long trousers and spraying boots, clothing and hat (but not skin!) with an insect repellent containing permethrin. Inspect yourself carefully after a walk for suspect black spots or itching. Remove any ticks very carefully using tweezers – be sure to get the head out – and disinfect the skin. Consult a doctor if you are concerned or experience any symptoms. For more information see www.lymeneteurope.org.

Birds

Birdwatchers will enjoy the small, delightful songsters in woods, as well as sizeable birds of prey such as kites, buzzards and golden eagles above the tree line. One special treat is the lammergeier or bearded vulture, back in the Alps after centuries of persecution. Easy to recognise for its orange neck ruff and impressive 3m wingspan, it glides low in search of an abandoned carcass; after extracting a bone it drops it on rocks to break it open for consumption.

BACKGROUND READING

Plenty of inspirational travel accounts from the mid 1800s and early 1900s are available in libraries and on the web and make for excellent reading. John Murray's *Handbook for Travellers in Southern Germany*, with its enthralling descriptions of the Dolomites, was a pioneering work from 1840. Later came the groundbreaking travelogue *The Dolomite Mountains: Excursions Through Tyrol, Carinthia, Carniola, and Friuli* by Josiah Gilbert and GC Churchill (1864). One of the best reads is Amelia Edwards' 1873 *Untrodden Peaks and Unfrequented Valleys: A Midsummer Ramble in the Dolomites*. Hard on its heels in 1875 came renowned mountaineer DW Freshfield's *Italian Alps: Sketches in the Mountains of Ticino, Lombardy, the Trentino, and Venetia*, which is especially poetic.

Of great interest for flower hunters is historic *The Dolomites* by Reginald Farrer (1913) as well as the modern-day Cicerone pocket guide *Alpine Flowers*, a valuable aid.

A joy to watch is the showy high-altitude wallcreeper, a bit like a woodpecker. Fluttering over extraordinarily sheer rock faces in its hunt for insects, it flashes its black plumage with red panels and white dots, attracting attention with its shrill piping call.

Probably the most memorable bird in the Dolomites is the cheeky scavenging alpine chough, a type of crow with a bright yellow-orange beak. Noisy flocks of these ubiquitous and gregarious birds perform acrobatics at high altitudes. Attracted by the slightest rustle of a food wrapper, they appear out of nowhere, hovering optimistically in the sure knowledge that all walkers stop at cols for a snack, leaving behind inevitable crumbs (and hopefully nothing else).

HOW TO GET THERE

The Dolomites are located in the northeast of Italy, not far from the border with Austria. The Alta Via 1 trek begins on their northernmost edge, at the lovely lake of Lago di Braies, also known by its German name Pragser Wildsee.

Note: All the access routes given below use a bus on the final leg. Due to the popularity of the lake, this bus may require booking in midsummer – check www.prags.bz.

By train to Monguelfo, then bus

A logical approach from northern Europe and the UK is by rail – a leisurely and less polluting option than flying. From London, one possible route is by Eurostar to Paris (www.eurostar.com) then TGV to Munich (www.sncf.com). Change here (www.

bahn.com) for Innsbruck then change for the Brenner Pass before alighting at Fortezza/Franzensfeste in Italy. Now you need the branch line (www.trenitalia.com) east to Monguelfo/Welsberg to pick up the SAD bus (www.sad.it) to Lago di Braies.

By air to Venice, then bus

Most walkers will be flying into Venice's Marco Polo airport (www.veniceairport.com). Direct buses (www.atvo.it or www.cortina express.it) whisk you straight to Cortina d'Ampezzo. From there, ongoing Cortina Express or SAD (www.sad.it) proceed to Dobbiaco/Toblach for the SAD bus to Lago di Braies.

By air to Treviso, then train and bus

Should your flight be scheduled into Treviso (www.trevisoairport.it), catch the local bus to Treviso railway station for a train (www.trenitalia.com) to Calalzo. Then pick up a Dolomiti Bus (https://dolomitibus.it) to Cortina. From there, ongoing Cortina Express (www.cortinaexpress.it) and SAD (www.sad.it) proceed to Dobbiaco/Toblach for the SAD bus to Lago di Braies.

By bus from Venice via Cortina

If your trip has started with a sojourn in Venice, catch the direct ATVO bus (www.atvo.it) from the Piazzale Roma bus station to Cortina d'Ampezzo. There, change to Cortina Express (www.cortinaexpress.it) or SAD (www.sad.it) for Dobbiaco/Toblach, where you need the Lago di Braies line.

By train from Venice, then bus

A further variant is the train from Venice (Venezia Santa Lucia) via Treviso to Calalzo, where you transfer to a Dolomiti Bus (https://dolomitibus.it) to Cortina. There, change to a Cortina Express (www.cortinaexpress.it) or SAD (www.sad.it) bus for Dobbiaco/Toblach, where you need the Lago di Braies service.

Private passenger and luggage transfers can be arranged through companies such as www.transferdolomiti.it, www.dolomititransfer.net, www.claudiobus.eu and www.taxialleghe.com.

Getting home

From the end of the Alta Via 1 at La Pissa, it's a 20min bus trip to the town of Belluno, with rail services south to

---

FROM VILLABASSA RAILWAY STATION ON FOOT

You can also walk in. The shortest route (2hr 30min) is from Villabassa railway station via the village of Ferrara. The description and GPX tracks are available on the Cicerone website: www.cicerone.co.uk/1081.

Venice. There are also trains north to Calalzo and ongoing buses for Cortina and Dobbiaco if you need to return to the trek start. Exit routes from intermediary points on the trail are mentioned in the route description.

Tickets

For Italian trains, unless you have a digital ticket and/or a booked seat – in which case your ticket will show a date and time – stamp your ticket in one of the machines on the platform before boarding. Failure to do so can result in a fine.

For buses, where possible, purchase tickets on websites or at ticket offices to save holding up the driver. When buying on board there may be a small surcharge.

WHEN TO GO

The Dolomites summer trekking season starts in mid June, when the huts open. This usually corresponds to a period when the last of the winter snow has melted off the paths, making for straightforward walking. July can be simply marvellous. Naturally, the situation varies year by year. To be on the safe side, if you're a beginner, you may be happier visiting in August. While this will mean busier paths and accommodation, rest assured that path conditions will be more favourable. Generally speaking, Italian alpine summers mean sunshine and heat, relieved by rain storms that build up during the day. While short and sweet, these may feature thunder and lightning.

Passo Giau and Ra Gusela (Stage 5)

September to October is the tail part of the Dolomites season and usually translates into crystal-clear skies, none of the summer humidity and haze, and quieter paths as fewer people are around; in short, perfect conditions. The downside is the vegetation, as the intense alpine green will have faded – but magical yellows and pre-autumn shades will be beginning. The chance of an odd storm and possibly a flurry or two of snow on high reaches is also on the cards. Lastly, you'll need to check that huts are still operating. Those in the northern Dolomites (the Südtirol region) tend to stay open longer (through to October) than those in the south, which shut in late September.

SHORTER ITINERARIES

The AV1 normally takes 11 days; however, shorter chunks are feasible if you have less time. Here are some suggestions. All the start and finish points are served by public transport (see the relevant points in the route description):

- four days from Lago di Braies (Stage 1) to Passo Falzarego (Stage 4), then bus to Cortina
- four days from Listolade (exit route in Stage 8) to La Pissa (Stage 11)
- five days from Cianzopè or Passo Falzarego (Stage 4) to Listolade (exit route in Stage 8) for bus to Belluno

- six days from Lago di Braies (Stage 1) to Passo Staulanza (Stage 6) and bus to Longarone.

ACCOMMODATION

Rifugi

Walkers can look forward to an excellent range of memorable places to sleep and eat on the AV1. An overnight stay in a Dolomites *rifugio* (*Hütte* in German, *Ücia* or *Ütia* in Ladin) is as essential as the walking experience. Cramped, rambling, cosy, modern, spartan… these hostel-like structures occupy amazing high-altitude spots. The majority belong to the Club Alpino Italiano (CAI), but lots are run by local families and alpine guides. The first huts were the work of far-seeing pioneers back in the late 1800s when Dolomites mountaineering was in its heyday. Thankfully since modernised, throughout the summer months they provide accommodation for walkers and climbers as well as excellent home-cooked meals and drinks all day, often served in a timber-lined *stube*, a room warmed by a traditional tiled stove. A *custode* or guardian is in residence during the opening period (generally June to September) and a staff member is always on duty to greet guests, deal with emergencies and satisfy needs – within reason. These jacks-of-all-trades also need to be good at chopping wood, baking cakes and even transporting supplies by rucksack if there's no cableway.

After checking in, guests need to leave their boots on the racks near the front door and change into sandals or hut slippers. Sleeping quarters range from 2–4-bed or bunk rooms up to a cavernous *dormitorio*. Duvets or blankets and a pillow are always provided, but guests must have their own sleeping sheet or bag liner – on sale in many huts. Smaller rooms with bed linen are sometimes available if you desire privacy – request a *camera*, but be aware that rooms *con bagno* (with en suite) are as rare as hen's teeth. Bathrooms are normally shared. Sparkling clean, they usually feature a couple of hand basins, mirrors and toilet cubicles (loo paper is always provided). You will need your own towel. Don't always expect a hot shower – especially in late summer when water shortages lead to restrictions. When on offer, it comes at a price and is usually timed, so be quick if you don't want to end up in a lather

you can't rinse off! It is safe to assume a hot shower is available unless otherwise specified in the accommodation listings.

You might consider rinsing out your day's gear; hang items outside on the clothes line unless there happens to be a drying room. Hint: don't leave your washing outside overnight as it will be soaked by dew. Several *rifugi* have installed washing machines – listed as laundry facilities in accommodation entries.

'Lights out' and silence are the rule between 10pm and 6am. The *rifugio* generator may be switched off, so keep your torch handy in case you need it during the night.

Meals are served at set times in a communal dining room that buzzes with mountain talk in different languages. If you have special dietary requirements, give the staff advance notice so they can cater for you. Gluten-free is *senza glutine*, I'm vegetarian/vegan is *sono vegetariana/ vegana* (or *vegetariano/vegano* for

WATER

Water is relatively scarce throughout the Dolomites due to the porous limestone and dolomite rock – which implies that most surface water disappears underground – as well as the dearth of glaciers and permanent snowfields. The bottom line is: use water sparingly and don't take it for granted. A general rule is to top up your water bottle whenever possible along the way. Tap water is *acqua da rubinetto*. It may occasionally not be drinkable – *acqua non potabile*. Safe bottled mineral water is always on sale, although this entails polluting transport and plastic bottles. Otherwise by all means carry a sterilising filter – there are all shapes and sizes on the market.

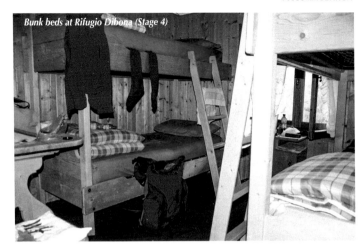

Bunk beds at Rifugio Dibona (Stage 4)

men). See the following section for food info.

No matter who a *rifugio* belongs to, anybody is welcome to stay – club membership is not compulsory. Rates vary according to the facilities offered. An average of €55 will cover *mezza pensione*/half board (three-course dinner, overnight stay, breakfast), not including drinks. It tends to be a very good deal, although naturally some saving can be made if you order individual meals. *Pernottamento* means an overnight stay with no meals. In the club-run huts, members (*soci*) of CAI and affiliated UIAA associations can count on saving at least €10.

Carry a good supply of euros in cash; there is only a single ATM en

---

ALPINE CLUBS

Membership of the CAI is open to all nationalities. Prospective members need to apply to individual branches; the complete list can be found at www.cai.it. The annual fee is around €50, with half-price rates for family members and 18 to 25-year-olds, and less for children. As well as reductions in huts throughout the Alps, this covers alpine rescue insurance. Otherwise Brits can join the UK branch of the Austrian club https://aacuk.org.uk, and for North Americans there's the Canadian Alpine Club www.alpineclubofcanada.ca and the US club https://americanalpineclub.org.

route (at Passo Falzarego, Stage 4) and detouring to a village uses up precious holiday time. Where possible, settle your bill in the evening to save wasting time in the morning. Many huts accept credit card payments – but check individual entries and never take it for granted.

Reservation is possible online as most huts have websites – full contact details can be found in the accommodation entries. A confirmation email is essential, and a deposit is often requested. Phone if in doubt. The AV1 has become popular with organised groups, so individuals are advised to book ahead. That said, some people go one day at a time. This is viable if you're versatile – many alternatives are listed. Refuge staff will always call ahead for you.

To phone from abroad, use the Italian country code +39 and include the initial '0' when dialling a land line. All of the refuges and hotels have a phone, occasionally only a mobile – recognisable by a number starting with '3'. An increasing number of huts now offer Wi-Fi.

Camping

No official campgrounds are encountered along the AV1, and wild camping is not permitted in any of the parks traversed (Stages 1–4, 9–11), with offenders risking fines. But where allowed, if you're prepared to carry the extra weight of a tent, sleeping bag and cooking gear along with supplementary water and food, a pitch under

the stars can be pure magic. Don't forget that level terrain is at a premium in the Dolomites. Furthermore, this route is not a stroll; you'll need to be fit and sufficiently experienced for long testing ascents and descents in alpine environments while shouldering a cumbersome rucksack. To camp in the vicinity of a *rifugio*, it's best to ask the staff; if allowed, they'll usually suggest a good spot. Naturally, you can partake of meals on the premises. Wherever you camp, be discreet, follow the 'dusk to dawn' rule and leave no trace.

There are no shops along the AV1 and unless you use the huts for meals and snacks, replenishing food supplies is not an easy task, requiring time-consuming detours. A glance at a map shows where a bus to shops can be caught: from Rifugio Pederü (Stage 2), Passo Falzarego (Stage 4) and Passo Staulanza (Stage 6).

FOOD AND DRINK

Meals are important in the day of a walker. All the *rifugi* along the way provide meals, snacks and refreshments, so you don't need to carry huge amounts of food.

Colazione or breakfast is generally continental style, with *caffè latte* (milk coffee) or *tè* (tea) to accompany bread, butter and jam, although cereals and yogurt, ham and cheese may also be on offer.

If you need a picnic lunch, staff are always happy to prepare rolls

Delicious casunziei pasta for dinner

(*panini*), but get your order in the evening before. Cheese is *formaggio* and *prosciutto* is ham. Otherwise, factor in lunch at an establishment en route. The menu will be similar to dinner, as follows.

Dinner (*cena*) generally means a choice of a first course (*primo piatto*), such as soup with vegetables (*minestrone*) or barley (*zuppa d'orzo*), or pasta with a meat (*ragù*) or tomato sauce (*al pomodoro*). If you're lucky there'll be *gnocchi di patate con ricotta affumicata* – delicate potato dumplings with smoked cheese – or Südtirol *canederli* – savoury bread dumplings flavoured with speck (smoked ham) and served in consommé or with melted butter. A Cortina district speciality is *casunziei* – tender ravioli with a beetroot filling, smothered in poppy seeds.

Second course is usually a serving of meat: *manzo* is beef, *maiale* pork, and *vitello* veal; *tagliata* is a type of steak. The flavoursome peppery sausage *pastin* hails from the Belluno district, as does *schiz*, a fresh local cheese similar to mozzarella that comes grilled or pan-fried in butter and cream.

Polenta is common – thick, steaming-hot cornmeal served with spicy meat stew goulash, *funghi* (wild mushrooms) or *formaggio fuso* (melted cheese). Always a good filler. A *frittata* (omelette) is an alternative, as are *uova con speck e patate* (fried eggs with speck and potatoes). Vegetables come as side dishes; fresh salad if you're lucky.

Dessert may be *frutti di bosco* – wild berries served with cake or ice cream. Other guaranteed standards

27

are homemade *crostata* (fruit tart) or *Apfelstrudel* – a luscious thin pastry case filled with layered sliced apple and spices. *Kaiserschmarrn* is a scrumptious Südtirol concoction of sliced pancake with sultanas, liberally sprinkled with icing sugar and spread with jam – a meal in itself.

Soft drinks and beer are always available, and some memorable wines hail from the Dolomites. Among the reds are full-bodied Teroldego and lighter Schiava from the Trentino, and excellent Lagrein and Blauburgunder (Pinot nero) from the slopes around Bolzano. The list of whites is headed by the aromatic Gewürztraminer, while very drinkable Rieslings are grown on steep terraces over the Isarco valley.

Lastly comes the fiery home-brewed *grappa*, served after dinner and flavoured with bilberries, sultanas, pine resin and unbelievably bitter gentian root. Remember that you need to get up and go walking tomorrow!

WHAT TO TAKE

The bottom line is you will need much less than you think. Basic items for personal comfort and gear to cover all weather extremes are essential, but be strict and remember you have to lug your stuff over the mountains for days on end. Safety is paramount: a heavy rucksack can become a hazard, putting tired walkers off-balance and leading to unpleasant falls and serious accidents.

Do you really need that paperback or weighty tablet? The 10pm 'lights out' rule precludes bedtime reading, and meal times can be profitable for trying out your language skills with other walkers and swapping track experiences.

The following checklist should help novice trekkers:

- comfortable boots with ankle support and non-slip Vibram-type sole
- rucksack – 35-litre capacity should do; plastic or stuff bags for separating contents
- light footwear such as sandals for evenings
- layers of clothing for dealing with conditions from scorching sun to a snow storm: t-shirts and shorts, comfortable long trousers (not jeans), warm fleece, a woolly hat and gloves (handy on cabled stretches)
- waterproofs – jacket, over-trousers and rucksack cover; otherwise a poncho
- whistle, small headlamp or torch for calling for help and exploring wartime tunnels
- lightweight sleeping sheet – silk is perfect
- small towel + personal toiletries
- mini first-aid kit and essential medicines
- high-energy snack food such as muesli bars
- maps and guidebook
- supply of euros in cash and credit/debit card

Typical AV1 waymarking

- telescopic trekking poles to help wonky knees on steep descents
- sunglasses, hat, chapstick and high-factor cream. For every 1000m you climb, the intensity of the sun's UV rays increases by 10%, augmented by reflection on snow. This, combined with lower levels of humidity and pollution which act as filters in other places, means you need a much higher protection factor cream than at sea level.
- water bottle or similar
- mobile phone, charger with adaptor
- camera, charger with adaptor
- foam ear plugs – they occupy next to no space and ensure a good night's sleep in a dormitory with snorers

MAPS

The maps in this book, at a scale of 1:75,000, show the route location and give information about important landmarks and geographical features. The map booklet (1:25,000) that accompanies this guide gives more detail.

As an alternative to the Kompass maps in the included map booklet, the Tabacco 1:25,000 *carta topografica per escursionisti* are also excellent. They can be consulted and ordered at www.tabaccoeditrice.com. Smartphone users can download Tabacco's app for digital maps at https://tabaccomapp.it. The hardcopy maps are sold throughout the Dolomites. Leading overseas booksellers include www.omnimap.com in the US and the Map Shop (www.themapshop.co.uk) or Stanfords (www.

stanfords.co.uk) in the UK, if you prefer to purchase them beforehand.

With slight overlaps, the following sheets are needed:

- 031 *Dolomiti di Braies* for Stages
  1–2
- 03 *Cortina d'Ampezzo e Dolomiti
  Ampezzane* for Stages 2–4 and
  first part of Stage 5
- 025 *Dolomiti di Zoldo, Cadorine
  e Agordine* for Stages 5 (second
  part) to 11.

The glossary in Appendix B
includes terminology found on maps.

LANGUAGES AND PLACE NAMES

In 1919, in the aftermath of the World
War 1 hostilities, the whole of the
Dolomites became Italian, forming
a fascinating cultural and linguistic
mosaic. Nowadays, in the northernmost Südtirol/Alto Adige region, 70%
of the population is German speaking
while the adjoining Trentino is mostly
Italian along with the remaining
southeastern chunk of the Dolomites,
the Veneto (where local dialects
abound). In addition, a significant
5% of these populations claim their
mother tongue as Ladin, an ancient
Rhaeto-Romanic language, pre-dating
the Latin brought by the Romans.
Maps and signposts can use three
versions of place names – a little con-
fusing for visitors. One to watch out
for is the Italian term *rifugio*, *Hütte*
in German, transformed into *Ücia* or
Ütia in Ladin. For the purposes of this

guidebook, to keep things simple and
to avoid crowding the text, Italian is
generally given precedence.

Be prepared for minor discrepancies between maps and signposts,
including the attached map booklet,
as changes are ongoing.

DOS AND DON'TS

It's better to arrive early and dry, than
late and wet.
Maxim for long-distance walkers

- Find time to get into good shape
  before setting out on your holiday, as it will maximise enjoy-
  ment. Remember that you'll be
  walking on alpine terrain which is
  never level, often steep and rocky,
  and occasionally exposed. You'll
  appreciate the scenery more if
  you're fit and healthy, and you'll
  react better in an emergency.
- Choose your footwear carefully.
  Avoid brand-new footwear (blis-
  ters!), but leave worn-out boots at
  home (slippery!).
- Apply the golden rule for rucksack preparation: 10% of your
  body weight + 2kg. Weigh in on
  the bathroom scales. Don't forget
  to make allowances for drinking water and food, and keep in
  mind that as the afternoon wears
  on and that hut seems ever further
  away, your pack will inexplicably
  get heavier.
- Carry protective clothing as well
  as energy foods for emergency

situations. Remember that in normal circumstances the temperature drops an average of 6°C for every 1000m you climb.

- Don't be overambitious. Read the walk description before setting out.

- Don't set out late on walks and always have extra time up your sleeve to allow for detours due to collapsed bridges, wrong turns and missing signposts. Plan on getting to your destination at an early hour in hot weather, as afternoon storms are not uncommon.

- Stick with your companions and don't lose sight of them. Remember that the progress of groups matches that of the slowest member.

- Learn the international call for help (see below).

- Check the weather forecast if possible – hut guardians are in the know. For the Südtirol see https://weather.provinz.bz.it, for Trentino see www.meteotrentino. it, and for the Veneto consult www.arpa.veneto.it. Never set out if conditions are bad. Even a broad track can become treacherous in adverse weather, and high-altitude terrain enveloped in thick mist makes orientation difficult.

- In electrical storms, don't shelter under trees or rock overhangs and keep away from metallic fixtures.

- Carry rubbish to a bin where it can be disposed of correctly; please don't push it under a rock.

Organic waste such as apple cores and orange peel should not be left lying around as it upsets the diet of animals and birds.

- Be considerate when making a toilet stop. Abandoned huts and rock overhangs could serve as life-saving shelter for someone. If you must use paper or tissues, carry it away; the small lightweight bags used by dog owners are perfect. There is no excuse for leaving unsightly toilet paper anywhere.

- Collecting flowers, insects or minerals is strictly forbidden everywhere, as is lighting fires.

- The Dolomites are in Italy – do make an effort to learn some Italian. All efforts will be hugely appreciated.

- Remember to collect the inked stamps from the *rifugi* you visit and present them to the Belluno Tourist Office at route's end for your badge and congratulations!

EMERGENCIES

For medical matters, walkers who live in the EU need a European Health Insurance Card (EHIC) while UK residents require a UK Global Health Insurance Card (GHIC). Holders of both are entitled to free or subsidised emergency treatment in Italy, which has an excellent public health system. Australia has a reciprocal agreement – see www.medicareaustralia.gov.au. Those from other countries should

Superb views are enjoyed near Forcella de Zita Sud (Stage 10)

make sure they have appropriate coverage.

Travel insurance to cover an alpine walking holiday is also strongly recommended, as costs in the case of rescue and repatriation can be hefty. Most Alpine Clubs cover their members for rescue operations – see box in 'Accommodation'.

Aiuto! (pronounced 'eye-yoo-toh') in Italian, and *Zu Hilfe!* (pronounced 'tsoo hilfer') in German, mean Help!

The international rescue signals can come in handy: the call for help is **six** signals per minute. These can be visual (such as waving a handkerchief or flashing a torch) or audible (whistling or shouting). Repeat after a one-minute pause. The answer is **three** visual or audible signals per minute, to be repeated after a one-minute

pause. Anyone who sees or hears a call for help must contact the nearest *rifugio* or police station as quickly as possible.

In Italy, the general emergency telephone number is 112, while calls for *soccorso alpino* (mountain rescue) need to be made to 118.

A final note, on mobile phones: it is tempting to be lulled into a false sense of security when carrying a mobile phone in the mountains. Be aware that relatively few high-alpine places have a signal. In contrast, all *rifugi* have a landline, mobile or satellite phone, and experienced staff can always be relied on in emergencies.

USING THIS GUIDE

This guide divides the AV1 into 11 handy stages that correspond to a reasonable day's walking, concluding at a *rifugio* with meals and accommodation. However, these are only suggestions, and the abundance of huts across the Dolomites means you can walk as much or as little as you like, varying stages and overnight stops at will.

Waymarking for the AV1 is '1' in a blue triangle, but where this is faded or missing, follow the local path numbers given in the route description. All paths are marked with an identifying number and red/white bars painted on prominent landmarks such as outcrops or trees, as well as signposts.

Throughout the route description, useful landmarks that feature on the accompanying stage map are given in **bold** with intermediary timing and altitude.

The info box at the beginning of each stage contains the following essential information:

Distance in kilometres. (This is nowhere near as important as height gain or loss.)

Total ascent in metres (NB 100m=328ft)

Total descent in metres

Grade gives an idea of the difficulty of the route. Remember that adverse weather conditions or snow cover will increase this. The grades used in this guide are as follows:

- **1:** a straightforward path with moderate gradient, suitable for all walkers (this corresponds to the Italian 'T', *Turistico*)

- **2:** a fairly strenuous alpine walk, but not especially difficult ('E', *Escursionistico* in Italian)

- **3:** experience on mountainous terrain is a prerequisite as there may be particularly steep and exposed sections; a head for heights and orientation skills will come in useful ('EE', *Escursionistico esperto* in Italian).

In terms of average overall difficulty, the AV1 rates Grade 2. One exception is in Stage 5 where there are short cable-aided stretches, but these are avoidable thanks to a variant. On the other hand, experienced walkers will enjoy branching out on Grade 3 variants: the Lagazuoi tunnels in Stage 4, as well as the Pelmo circuit in Stage 6.

Time is approximate and does not include pauses for picnics, admiring views, photos and nature stops, so always add on a couple of hours to be realistic. Everyone walks at a different pace.

GPX tracks

GPX tracks for the route in this guidebook are available to download free at www.cicerone.co.uk/1081/GPX. If you have not bought the book through the Cicerone website, or have bought the book without opening an account, please register your purchase in your Cicerone library to access GPX and update information.

A GPS device is an excellent aid to navigation, but you should also carry a map and compass and know how

Bustling Rifugio Pederü in glacially formed Val dai Tamersc (Stage 2)

to use them. GPX files are provided in good faith, but in view of the profusion of formats and devices, neither the author nor the publisher accepts responsibility for their use. We provide files in a single standard GPX format that works on most devices and systems, but you may need to convert files to your preferred format using a GPX converter such as gpsvisualizer.com or one of the many other apps and online converters available.

ALTA VIA 1

The magnificent Moiazza Sud appears at Forcella del Camp (Stage 8)

Dolomite silhouettes on the way to Rifugio Coldai (Stage 6)

Before setting out on this adventure, trekkers arriving from afar after a long journey may prefer to spend a night in the proximity of the Alta Via 1 start. Some suggestions are given here.

Whatever direction you arrive from, you'll travel along a bit of the major road and train artery, Val Pusteria. At its eastern end, the handy transport hub town of Dobbiaco has a youth hostel (tel 0474 976216, http://dobbiaco.ostello.bz, with left luggage facilities), along with hotels (tourist info tel 0474 972132, www.hochpustertal.info/en), ATM and shops. Monguelfo and Villabassa also have places to stay and facilities.

However, continuing on the approach route, there is accommodation closer to the lakeside trek start. Breaking off south from Val Pusteria is Valle di Braies, named for 'trousers' as the valley forks into 'legs', each with neat farming settlements and manicured meadows. The village Ferrara (Braies di Dentro) has a bus stop, groceries and guesthouses including Gasthof Huber (tel 0474 748670, www.gasthof-huber.it) and Garni Bergblick (tel 392 1966953, www.bergblick.bz), as well as a tourist office nearby (tel 0474 748660 www.prags.bz/en).

Further on, 3km west, is Hotel Steinerhof (tel 0474 748649, www. hotel-steinerhof-pustertal.com). Now a mere handful of kilometres are all that separate you from the valley conclusion and the beautiful emerald-green Lago di Braies. This is where the AV1 begins its memorable journey.

Alongside vast fee-paying car parks, a café, souvenir shop and WCs stands a marvellous alpine Grand Hotel, built in 1899 and famous for hosting the Beatles' personal guru Maharishi Mahesh Yogi in the 1960s. The art nouveau premises make a splendid (albeit pricey) place to stay: Hotel Lago di Braies (tel 0474 748602, www.lagodibraies.com).

STAGE 1
Lago di Braies to Rifugio Biella

Start	Lago di Braies
Distance	6km
Total ascent	870m
Total descent	60m
Grade	2
Time	3hr 20min

In the realms of the Parco Naturale Fanes-Senes-Braies, this thrilling opening to the Alta Via 1 starts at a beautiful alpine lake set amid pine forest and soaring Dolomite peaks. It entails a problem-free, steady (if tiring) climb to a high-altitude plateau that rewards walkers with wide-reaching vistas. Those with energy to burn and a head for heights might want to fit in the Grade 2–3 ascent of 2810m Croda del Beco, which flanks the hut at stage end – see below. On the other hand, those desirous of a guesthouse – as opposed to the excellent but spartan Rifugio Biella – may choose to proceed a further 1hr to Rifugio Sennes (see Stage 2).

Formed when the valley was obstructed by an ancient rock fall, **Lago di Braies** lies at the foot of sheer, towering **Croda del Beco** – a 'gigantic elephant uprearing itself' as described by the visiting Englishmen Gilbert and Churchill in 1864. In the Ladin language this is known as Sas dla Porta, 'gateway rock'. According to an ancient saga, once every hundred years, on a night with full moon, two women emerge through a secret doorway in the mountain. Leaving their subjects to slumber in rocky caverns, Princess Dolasilla rows her blind mother the Queen of Fanes across the lake, listening out for silver trumpets to announce the dawning of a new age for their doomed kingdom. In vain for the time being, it would seem.

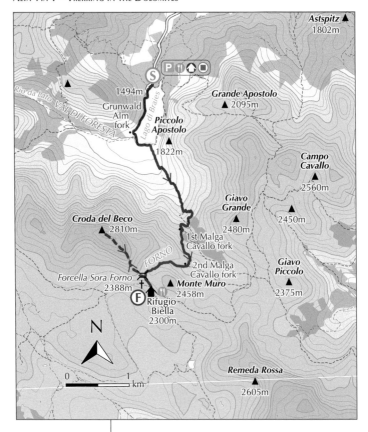

Popular for old-style boating and the set for aptly named Italian soap opera *Un passo dal cielo* ('One step from heaven'), the lake's crystal-clear waters are bordered by shingle beaches. Think twice about taking the plunge, though: the low temperatures are discouraging – the surface rarely exceeds 14°C. It begins to ice over around November, reverting to liquid form in May. Notwithstanding, trout survive in the chilly depths.

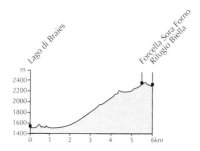

At **Hotel Lago di Braies** (1494m) go R, flanking the buildings, for the broad white gravel path (n.1) that soon heads S past a chapel. It leads along the lake's west bank, with the massive bulk of the Croda del Beco ahead. This pretty stretch traverses squirrel-ridden woods close to the water's edge, the opposite shore dominated by the Grande and Piccolo Apostolo.

Close to an attractive beach, ignore the **fork** R for path n.19 to Grünwald Alm in Val di Foresta and curve

Lovely Lago di Braies

SE, sticking to the lakeside. Further around the shore, AV1 leaves this paradise, forking SSE (1496m, **30min**) for the start of the 870m climb.

The well-trodden path traverses vast rivers of scree colonised in patches by dwarf mountain pine, bilberry shrubs and mountain avens. You wind steadily upwards, reaching wooden steps and a cable attached to a rock face. Not far up, ignore a first **fork** for Malga Cavallo. Pretty, shady wood precedes entry into a vast rock-strewn amphitheatre. Here an imposingly steep barrier is surmounted on a zigzag path aided by cables, helpful in wet or icy conditions. ◄

The sheer rock flanks carry clear signs of karstification, in the shape of grooves left by rainwater.

Ignore a second Malga Cavallo **fork** (2186m) and take an abrupt branch R (W) which marks the entry into the so-called *forno* (oven) – a heat trap, as will quickly

Cables help walkers up steep sections of the trail

become evident to midsummer walkers. The clear path weaves its way between toppled rocks at the foot of Monte Muro on the final leg to the pass **Forcella Sora Forno** (2388m, **2hr 40min**) and a shrine.

Entering the Parco Naturale delle Dolomiti d'Ampezzo, the panorama is vast and breathtaking, from the most northerly Dolomite peak of Sass de Putia, across to the glittering glaciated Marmolada, taking in the Tofane pyramids and Pelmo to the south. For those who feel up to it and are not bothered by exposure, the optional rewarding Grade 2–3 ascent of Croda del Beco begins here.

Side trip to Croda del Beco (2hr return)

From the pass, a zigzagging path NW tackles an exposed corner with the help of cables set into the rock face. There are soon bird's-eye views onto Rifugio Biella. The flattish mountain top will come as quite a surprise, as will the reticent ibex that graze here in summer. Over on the northern edge is the dizzy summit cross of Croda del Beco (2810m) directly over Lago di Braies. Simply breathtaking. Return the same way, taking special care on the exposed corner ridge.

From the *forcella*, a short way down the slope is **Rifugio Biella** (2300m, **10min**).

> **Rifugio Biella**, aka Seekofel Hütte (tel 0436 866991, rifugiobiella@libero.it, sleeps 46, open third week June to end Sept, credit cards can be used – but only when the weather is fair and the landline is working!). This friendly, well-run hut has generous traditional meals and a self-serve breakfast; the timber-lined dorms are cosy with basic facilities – expect a cold shower.

STAGE 2
Rifugio Biella to Rifugio Fanes

Start	Rifugio Biella
Distance	13km
Total ascent	710m
Total descent	980m
Grade	1
Time	4hr 30min

Today the AV1 crosses undulating rocky terrain on easy paths and 4WD tracks constructed for military supply purposes during World War 1. Several lovely *rifugi* are touched on before a plunge to a roadhead, which entails losing an awful lot of height. Here is a modern hut where refreshments are probably in order as you need to gird your loins – the day concludes with an extended uphill stretch, terminating in a beautiful pasture basin with a choice of comfortable lodgings. Walkers desirous of an overnight stay at a smaller establishment can continue on an extra 45min to Malga Fanes Grande in Stage 3.

From **Rifugio Biella** (2300m) set out W along the jeep route (n.6) in gentle descent below the remarkable onion layers of the southeast face of Croda del Beco. Just 10min on, AV1 parts ways with the track. It branches R uphill (SW) on path n.6A, crossing knobbly grassy terrain punctuated with marmot burrows to reach the 2300m level. Re-entering the Parco Naturale Fanes-Senes-Braies, it drops to join another jeep track, thence L to reach comfortable **Rifugio Sennes** (2116m, **1hr**).

Rifugio Sennes (tel 0474 646355 or 328 7945579, www.sennes.com, sleeps 65 in rooms and dorms, open early June to mid Oct, credit cards accepted).

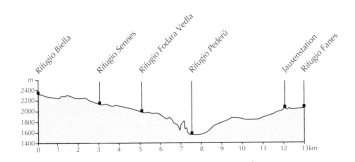

Past the huddle of photogenic wood-tile-roofed shepherds' huts, the jeep track (n.7) proceeds S. Keep R at the first fork, marked by a crucifix. The path drops to rejoin the track – go R, heading SW over Plan de Lasta, thick with dwarf mountain pines and dotted with larch. Soon AV1/n.7 forks L to ramble through lovely woodland, dropping to a dirt road. A stroll L are old timber huts, a tiny chapel and **Rifugio Fodara Vedla** (1966m, **40min**).

The woodland path after Rifugio Fodara Vedla

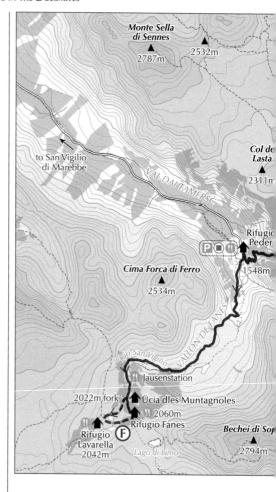

Rifugio Fodara Vedla (tel 0474 501093, www.
fodara.it, sleeps 36 in rooms and dorm, open
June to Oct, credit cards accepted) This spacious
family-run hotel-grade establishment occupies an
enchanting position.

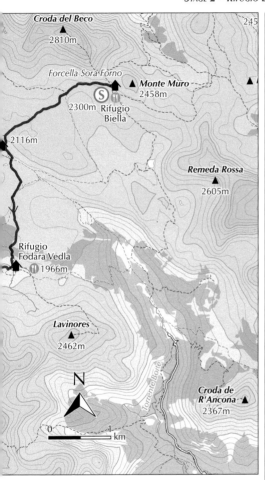

Now n.7 dips across a stream before branching R on a path that soon traverses high over an awesome gully. An easy descent through larch wood comes to a track junction, where you fork L for a knee-jarring white dirt road via a precipitous gully. ▶ Below in the glacial

Due west over the valley is jagged Cima Forca di Ferro, bright red for its iron content (ferro).

45

U-shaped Val dai Tamersc is bustling modern café-guest-house Rifugio Pederü (1548m, **50min**).

> **Rifugio Pederü** (tel 0474 834316, www.pederue. it, sleeps 24 in rooms and dorm, open June to Oct, credit cards accepted).

Exit
Summer SAD buses run to San Vigilio di Marebbe (tourist info tel 0474 501037, www.sanvigilio.com, shops, ATM, hotels).

Next point your boots S. Path n.7 branches R across the stream to climb the valley side with its immense erosive spills colonised by dwarf mountain pine. A dirt road is touched on briefly, then you veer R over a rise. Amid low bushy vegetation, the unsurfaced road is joined once and for all at the 2000m mark above the gushing stream **Rio San Vigilio**.

An uphill stretch S past an inviting **Jausenstation** (café) leads into a beautiful pasture basin. Dotted with old dark timber hay chalets and flanked by curious limestone slab terracing with conifers, it is known as the 'Marmot's Parliament' – a reference to the long-gone era of the legendary Kingdom of Fanes (see Stage 1 story).

> **Ücia dles Muntagnoles** (tel 347 5214753, www. muntagnoles.com, sleeps 11 in rooms, open mid June to early Oct). This old herder's hut has been converted into simple accommodation for walkers, with meals.

Here, at a **fork** (2022m), take the L branch leading to **Rifugio Fanes** (2060m, **2hr**).

> **Rifugio Fanes** (tel 0474 453001, www.rifugiofanes. com, sleeps 60 in rooms and dorms, open mid June to mid Oct, credit cards accepted). This popular rambling establishment has been beautifully

modernised and enlarged and offers accommodation for all pockets.

Detour to Rifugio Lavarella

From the 2022m fork in the road, continue straight on (SW) for 5min past a reedy lake to the peaceful, family-run **Rifugio Lavarella** (2042m).

> **Rifugio Lavarella** (tel 0474 501094 or 0474 501079, www.lavarella.it, sleeps 45 in rooms and dorms, open June to Oct, credit cards accepted). Visitors should be aware that the basement of the building has been converted into a micro-brewery – the highest in the Dolomites! At the rear of the building rises the gently sloping Sasso della Croce formation that culminates in Sasso delle Dieci and Sasso delle Nove.

The next day, take the path crossing the lake emissary and go up NE through wood to join the track just above **Rifugio Fanes** – an extra 15min.

The link from Rifugio Lavarella back to the main route

STAGE 3
Rifugio Fanes to Rifugio Lagazuoi

Start	Rifugio Fanes
Distance	12.2km
Total ascent	1150m
Total descent	450m
Grade	2
Time	5hr 30min

A laidback stroll along historic military tracks and across undulating stony pasture uplands becomes, little by little, more enthralling as all manner of Dolomites are approached. The Forcella del Lago marks AV1's entry into the dramatic and breathtaking Cortina Dolomites (although it hasn't been too bad so far!). A steep gully is navigated on a much-improved path; an easier but slightly longer variant via Rifugio Scotoni is also given (walkers who opt for it may prefer to overnight there and continue with AV1 the following day). A tiring climb through what amounts to an open-air World War 1 museum concludes at Rifugio Lagazuoi. And yes, it is worth all the effort as this is an unrivalled vantage point when the weather is clear.

From **Rifugio Fanes** (2060m), path n.11 cuts the curves of the wide white gravel track and heads SE up to the open grassy **Passo di Limo** (2175m) with its old wood cross. ◄ After passing Lago di Limo, near abandoned World War 1 barracks and trenches, AV1 breaks off R. This soon slots into a track heading S with an inspiring outlook to spiral-form Cime Ciampestrin and Vallon Bianco. Not far on is **Malga Fanes Grande** (2156m, **45min**).

This spot affords great views west to Sasso della Croce.

Malga Fanes Grande aka Ütia de Gran Fanes (tel 346 2193374, the spacious attic has mattresses for 12, open mid June to late Sept, no shower). This

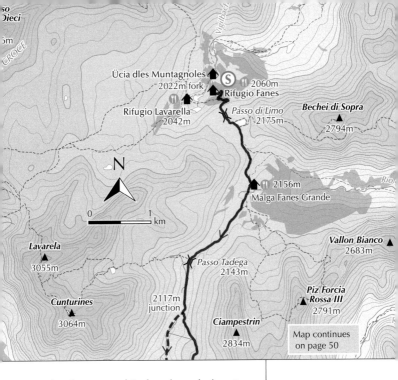

welcoming summer dairy farm does refreshments and simple meals al fresco or in a lovely timber-lined *stube*.

Now with the massive Cunturines ahead and even a peek of the snowbound Marmolada, AV1 proceeds SW on the wide track n.11 across undulating pasture accompanied by a trickling stream, marmots and cows. Close to a turn-off for the Cunturines peak is imperceptible **Passo Tadega** (2143m). A short distance S is a strategic if unnamed **junction** (2117m, **45min**), where AV1 breaks off L on n.20B.

Variant via Capanna Alpina and Rifugio Scotoni
A lovely, slightly easier (and only 15min longer) route, n.11 at first continues as a wide track up and down and

across a stream, to the marvellous lookout **Col Locia** (2069m). Next, flanking a chasm, the path plunges SW in zigzags below awesome cliffs. Watch your step on the loose stones. Finally, down on Plan de la Forca in lovely woodland, it levels out and crosses a bridge. Not far on is a signed fork (1725m), where it is possible to exit the route (see below).

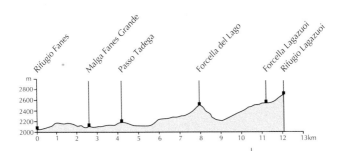

Go L (SE) here on n.20. The jeep track is a steady, problem-free climb to the beautiful plateau housing the friendly **Rifugio Scotoni** (1985m, **50min**).

> **Rifugio Scotoni** (tel 0471 847330, www.scotoni.it, sleeps 20 in comfortable rooms, open mid June to early Oct, credit cards accepted). It is a magnet for visitors thanks to its excellent traditional food featuring flavoursome local speck and grilled meats.

Path n.20 then continues uphill to Lago di Lagazuoi, and shortly afterwards joins the main AV1 route (**30min**).

Exit

To leave the route, from the 1725m fork, walk on to nearby café-restaurant **Capanna Alpina** (1726m) and follow signs for **Saré**/Sciaré (1652m), a further 20min away on the Valparola–San Cassiano road. Here is a camping ground, eateries and bus stops for SAD or Cortina Express summer runs in both directions.

Main route

From the unnamed junction at 2117m the clear path climbs steadily with stunning views to far-off Sella and Marmolada (explored on Alta Via 2). You're heading for a notch between Cima del Lago and Cima Scotoni, namely **Forcella del Lago** (2486m, **45min**). The reward is a great view ahead to the smooth profile of Piccolo Lagazuoi.

AV1 climbs over the vast expanse of the Alpe di Lagazuoi

This is where the variant from Rifugio Scotoni rejoins the main AV1 route.

However, at your feet a plunging, stomach-dropping gully is revealed. But fear not: the regularly restored path is good, if narrow. It zigzags madly downhill, aided by sturdy timber reinforcements. Below lies the glittering green Lago di Lagazuoi.

Eventually exit the gully, keeping L (S), high above the lake. Ignore the turn-offs R and traverse scree to the bleached stone ruins of a World War 1 building. Here, at approx. 2220m, turn L onto the broad path n.20. ◄

You now find yourself on the Alpe di Lagazuoi, an immense grey rock incline where chamois graze. Enclosed by the walls of Lagazuoi Grande and Piccolo Lagazuoi, this was a key arena during the 1915–18 conflict. Scattered timbers, remains of trench systems and even cabins for an aerial goods cableway bear witness to the folly. These will serve as distractions from the stiff ascent that awaits to today's destination: half a vertical kilometre ahead – and it never feels closer over the next hour or so!

Edged with stone blocks, the wartime track enters the Parco Naturale delle Dolomiti d'Ampezzo and touches on a ghost village, military huts all but crumbled to the ground. You emerge at last at **Forcella Lagazuoi** (2573m, **1hr 50min**).

Turn R for the final slog: tight zigzags up the side of a bulldozed winter ski piste, past caverns dating back to World War 1. A tad above the cable-car station is the superb **Rifugio Lagazuoi** (2752m, **40min**) – the highest point on AV1.

Rifugio Lagazuoi (tel 0436 867303 or 340 7195306, www.rifugiolagazuoi.com, sleeps 76 in lovely spacious rooms and dorms, open early June to mid Oct, credit cards accepted). Clouds permitting, the renowned panoramic terrace will provide breathtaking views to enjoy with that well-earned beer.

The final steep piste, climbing towards Rifugio Lagazuoi

A final temptation awaits...

Extension to Piccolo Lagazuoi (30min return)
From the *rifugio* terrace, a clear path with a guiding handrail proceeds WNW along a narrow ridge at first. The way broadens, culminating at a huge cross marking the actual peak of **Piccolo Lagazuoi** (2778m). This sees you an impressive 26m above the highest point on the trek!

STAGE 4
Rifugio Lagazuoi to Rifugio Nuvolau

Start	Rifugio Lagazuoi
Distance	12.8km
Total ascent	1100m
Total descent	1275m
Grade	2
Time	5hr 30min

Whichever way you go, this stage is of great interest for both the spectacular mountains and the abundant reminders of the terrible years of World War 1, due to the vicinity of the former Austrian-Italian border. The main AV1 route embarks on a memorable traverse below the awesome Tofana de Rozes. Beyond a hospitable *rifugio* it drops to the Cortina–Passo Falzarego road then climbs through forest to the fascinating, renowned Cinque Torri area, with a magnificent conclusion at lookout par excellence Nuvolau. The way is dotted with comfortable *rifugi*, should you prefer a shorter day.

However, there are difficult decisions to be made! For sure-footed walkers with a sense of adventure and no vertigo or claustrophobia, a strongly recommended Grade 3 variant explores the Lagazuoi wartime rock tunnels, cutting dramatically down to Passo Falzarego (headtorch necessary, gloves recommended). Afterwards is a fair climb, skirting the Averau to reach a cosy *rifugio* where the main route is joined for the final leg to Nuvolau. Finally, a variant descent is offered to Passo Giau.

WAR TUNNELS

During the 1914–18 conflict, Piccolo Lagazuoi was occupied by the troops of the Austro-Hungarian Empire – it is important to remember that Cortina d'Ampezzo was one of the southernmost parts of that empire at the time, so this was the front for the advancing Italians. Both sides spent massive amounts of time, energy and human life excavating daring tunnels (11 in all) through the mountains to lay explosives mining enemy positions. The scars can still be seen – chilling reminders of the ordeal both sides endured; more lives were lost through avalanches than actual fighting. The tunnels have been restored for visitors, with helpful info boards illustrating living conditions and supply routes. The variant route follows the Galleria Lagazuoi: 1100m-long, maximum 45-degree gradient, 230m in descent. Excavated by the Italians from their stronghold on the Cengia Martini ledge, it was designed to dislodge the Austrians from the summit above.

Variant via wartime tunnels and Passo Falzarego to Rifugio Averau (3hr)

Walkers must be equipped with a headlamp; gloves can also be handy as the cable handrail is cold. For a modest

The entrance to the Lagazuoi wartime tunnels

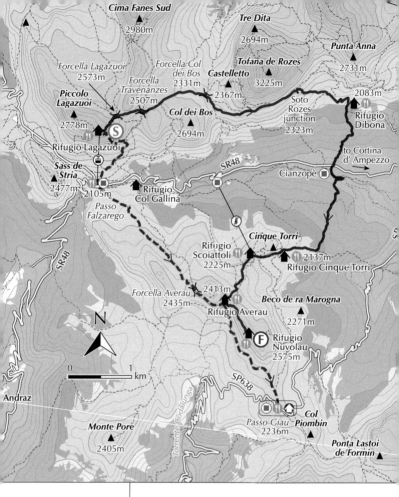

fee you may prefer to send your rucksack down to Passo
Falzarego by cable-car.

From **Rifugio Lagazuoi** (2752m) walk down the steps
to the cable-car station then follow the arrows for *galleria* (tunnel), leading below the concrete platform and
L (E) via trenches and a narrow crest. The actual tunnel
entrance is a timber doorway where the path 'disappears'

into a hole. A glance down into the semi-darkness gives a good idea of what's to come!

The cable handrail is reassuring as it's often slippery underfoot, especially on the steps and ladders. A string of rock 'windows' provide dizzying views and occasional natural light. En route are reconstructed storage depots, cramped sleeping quarters and eerie passageways.

After an hour of knee-jarring descent, you exit onto a broad ledge adjoining Cengia Martini. Proceed L via a snow-choked gully and final short tunnel, then zigzag down to join path n.402 for the final drop to the road at well-visited **Passo Falzarego** (2105m, **1hr 30min**), where you'll find an ATM, cafés, restaurants and tantalising souvenirs the likes of miniature marmot key rings. The route can be exited here (see below). The closest accommodation is 10min down the road (Cortina direction, 2054m).

> **Rifugio Col Gallina** (tel 0436 2939 or 339 4425105, www.rifugiocolgallina.com, sleeps 40 in rooms, open mid June to late Sept, credit cards accepted).

On the opposite side of the pass, path n.441 strikes out SE across red clay slopes and flowered meadows. Further uphill, rocky terrain is encountered and the going gets steeper via a series of gullies. Stick with n.441 over a ridge and join a wider path R to emerge at **Forcella Averau** (2435m, **1hr 10min**), haunt of amazing numbers of jet-black alpine choughs.

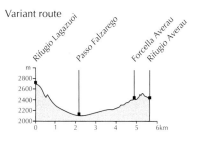

Variant route

Now you take the scree path SE skirting the crumbling southern wall of Averau, accompanied by vast panoramas all the way to Forcella Nuvolau. Here you encounter **Rifugio Averau** (2413m, **20min**), and the main AV1 route.

Exit
Passo Falzarego (see variant above) has buses to Val Badia (SAD, Cortina Express), Cortina d'Ampezzo and Belluno (Dolomiti Bus).

Main route
From **Rifugio Lagazuoi** (2752m) retrace your steps down to **Forcella Lagazuoi** (2573m) and turn R onto n.402–1 beneath a stark red mountainside and heavy-duty avalanche barriers. Ahead rise the massive Tofane. You quickly reach **Forcella Travenanzes** (2507m) and an exit path for Passo Falzarego. However, AV1 proceeds across the head of the immense trough of Val Travenanzes, ignoring turn-offs. Grassy-stony terrain is traversed in slight descent to **Forcella Col dei Bos** (2331m, **1hr 15min**) with its World War 1 memorial hung with rusty barbed wire. ◄

Fork R on n.402 in gradual descent along the lines of trenches. Confusingly, more signs announce Forcella Col dei Bos at slightly lower altitudes. At the third (2290m) sign, turn L (E) on n.404. Climbing a little, it skirts the

Towering overhead is the ill-famed Castelletto spur, hotly contested during the war and devastated by explosives in the summer of 1916, resulting in huge loss of life.

Main route

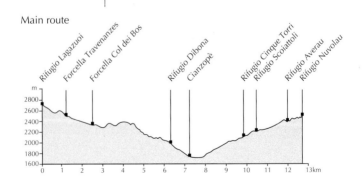

awesome southern base of the Tofana de Rozes, and you ignore a branch L (2400m) for the Galleria del Castelletto. The path narrows and is a little exposed as it cuts across steep scree flanks with constant minor ups and downs. Watch your step.

Further along, at the **Soto Rozes junction** (2323m) just below the Tofana Grotta (cave), leave this incredibly scenic path and fork R. A zigzagging plunge through dwarf mountain pines concludes on a track near a cableway loading point. Keep L for the Valon de Tofana junction (2120m) then continue SE in gentle descent on the jeep track to the beautifully located **Rifugio Dibona** (2083m, **1hr 15min**).

After Forcella Lagazuoi you face the massive Tofane

Rifugio Dibona (tel 0436 860294 or 333 143 4408, rifugiodibona@gmail.com, sleeps 64, open mid June to late Sept, credit cards accepted). Named after Angelo Dibona, a famous local turn-of-the-century guide and mountaineer, the well-run hut and renowned eatery serves as a strategic base for climbers on the Tofane.

Here you'll find a new gondola lift overhead and bus stops for both directions.

Down the concrete road, fork R on n.442 at the first bend. The steep descent path traverses beautiful conifer wood with roe deer and clearings of meadow saffron, finally reaching the Cortina–Passo Falzarego road at **Cianzopè** (1724m, **35min**). ◄

Cross straight over and take the narrow surfaced road, n.439, into woodland. Not far up, as a signed path, n.439 breaks off to climb S steadily albeit steeply through the trees. It eventually emerges on the edge of an ancient landslide – a superb viewing point over the Cortina basin. At a broader old paved track, turn R (W) for the final leg to cosy old-style **Rifugio Cinque Torri** (2137m, **1hr 10min**).

Rifugio Cinque Torri (tel 0436 2902, **www.rifugio 5torri.it**, sleeps 24, open mid June to late Sept, credit cards accepted). Popular with climbers, it excels in soft duvets, not to mention local cuisine such as luscious *casunziei* – pasta parcels with beetroot and poppy seeds.

Sadly, in 2004 one of the minor towers dramatically collapsed.

It's worth allowing extra time here to explore the maze of World War 1 fortifications and snaking trenches at the northern foot of the crazy Cinque Torri (five towers), where acrobatic rock climbers put on spectacular performances. ◄

Continue uphill to the splendidly placed and cheery **Rifugio Scoiattoli** (2225m, **10min**).

Rifugio Scoiattoli (tel 0436 867939 or 333 8146960, **www.rifugioscoiattoli.it**, sleeps 42 in comfortable rooms and dorm, open mid June to end Sept, credit cards accepted). The name 'squirrels' is for the famous Cortina team of climbers. A chair lift from the road below comes up this far.

The wartime tunnels variant rejoins here.

Now as a straightforward broad track, n.439 leads essentially SSE up to the saddle that is home to **Rifugio Averau** (2413m). ◄

Rifugio Averau (tel 0436 4660 or 335 6868066, **www.rifugioaverau.it**, sleeps 42 in rooms and dorm, open beg June to end Sept, credit cards accepted, laundry facilities available). Memorable meals are served on an open terrace with brilliant views to the Marmolada and its shrinking glacier.

Walkers who would prefer to avoid the aided sections at the start of Stage 5 should turn off here for the low, shorter variant to Passo Giau. But do go up the Nuvolau first – you won't regret it! (Allow 1hr up and back.)

Lower variant to Passo Giau (50min)
From Rifugio Averau n.452 drops S on a lane before branching L to coast SE beneath Nuvolau. You cross loose scree and grassy slopes, home to a playful colony of marmots. At the foot of the soaring rocky point of Ra Gusela, and a short way above the road pass, is a junction (2244m) where you meet up with the main AV1 route for the final metres in gentle descent to **Passo Giau** (2236m, **50min**) – see Stage 5.

The wonderfully panoramic path to Rifugio Nuvolau

Uphill of Rifugio Averau a path climbs quickly to join the broad Nuvolau ridge. Here popular n.439 follows the bare rock incline SE, for the final steep slog to the amazing perch of **Rifugio Nuvolau** (2575m, **1hr 15min**).

> **Rifugio Nuvolau** (tel 0436 867938, **www. rifugionuvolau.it**, CAI, sleeps 25, open mid June to end Sept, credit cards accepted). While creature comforts are scarce – don't expect a shower, let alone hot water – the extraordinary position and hospitality make up for it. Waking up for the dawn colours is a must, especially if the mount is not living up to its name – *nuvola* means 'cloud'. The very first hut in the Dolomites, it was inaugurated in 1883 thanks to a donation left by a wealthy baron from Dresden in recognition for help in recovering from a serious illness. All but destroyed by artillery during World War 1, it had to be rebuilt by the local Alpine Club. A bridle track opened the way for fashionable ladies on horseback. And the views? Not enough space here to list them all.

Rifugio Nuvolau on its perch

STAGE 5
Rifugio Nuvolau to Rifugio Città di Fiume

Start	Rifugio Nuvolau
Distance	12.8km
Total ascent	500m
Total descent	1200m
Grade	2–3
Time	5hr

Quite an amazing series of Dolomite landscapes are encountered today in a superb succession of peaks and ranges. The stage begins with several short vertical aided passages of average difficulty and exposure to get you over the rocky realms of the Nuvolau. Only set out in good weather and without a bulky rucksack. If you have any qualms at all, return to Rifugio Averau and go for the straightforward variant to Passo Giau – see Stage 4.

After crossing the road at Passo Giau, a few more moderate climbs lead to a magnificent open basin of emerald pasture, once the hunting ground of Mesolithic men. The panoramas are non-stop as a brilliant line-up of Dolomites comes into view – the Tofane are left behind, the Pelmo is the undisputed king of the day, but the Civetta comes a close second at the stage end. Walkers in need of mod cons and a bit of luxury should plan on overshooting Rifugio Città di Fiume by an extra 1hr 15min, to overnight at Passo Staulanza – see Stage 6.

From **Rifugio Nuvolau** (2575m), just past the flagpole, path n.438 disappears over the edge of the short ridge. It drops with the aid of firmly anchored cable, ending with a short ladder, to easier terrain. With an eye out for red/white waymarking, head SE across undulating rock, ignoring a higher route to the Ra Gusela summit. A pole at the far edge of the plateau marks the start of a second aided section, beginning with a brief ledge and descending a crumbly, moderately exposed gully with more cable.

The final crumbly gully descent below Nuvolau

The path continues in steep descent on loose stones. Watch your step. At a **junction** (Forame, 2172m) branch R on n.443. It's a saunter through cow-grazed land before the variant from Rifugio Averau slots in and together

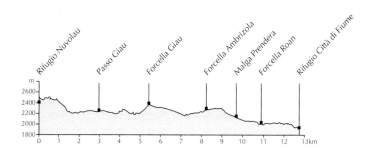

65

you join the bikers at **Passo Giau** (2236m, **1hr 30min**), where you'll find a coffee shop, restaurant and the pricey Rifugio Passo Giau.

> **Rifugio Passo Giau** (tel 346 0696745, www. passogiau.it, sleeps 17 in rooms, open June to Sept).

Exit
Summer Dolomiti Bus to Cortina.

Cross the road for path n.436 below a chapel, and begin the gentle ascent to the rear of a grassy knoll to reach **Forcella de Col Piombin** (2236m), the name from 'lead' for a long-gone mine. Mostly E now, the narrow way drops briefly across the head of a grazing valley, cutting over strata of the coral atoll covered with volcanic material that make up adjacent Monte Cernera.

At a conspicuous fault line with gashes of dramatically contrasting rocks, you embark on a puff-inducing ascent R (S) that sees you clamber out at **Forcella Giau** (2360m, **1hr**). Bid farewell to the Tofane and direct your gaze to the rearing Pelmo. The AV1 now keeps L (mostly E) on the edge of the rich pastures of **Mondeval di Sora**.

> **Mesolithic hunters** were known to have closed off the five passes entering this basin to trap wild animals such as elk, ibex and deer in combined tribal summer hunts. Evidence of settlement was unearthed at a landmark boulder.

Here the vast outlook takes in the Cortina basin, dominated by the Pomagagnon and adjoining Cristallo. Close at hand is the jagged, toothy Croda da Lago.

The path proceeds under the sheer southern face of the Lastoi de Formin, where chattering choughs and felt-leaved edelweiss abound. You dip to cross streams and are dwarfed by soaring Cima di Ambrizola as you gain the earthy saddle **Forcella Ambrizola** (2277m, **1hr**). ◄

Still on n.436, coast R (S) amid a chaos of fallen rocks and boulders below towering Beco de Mezodì to the minor pass of **Forcella Col Duro**, where cows hang out. A gentle descent leads to the stalls of **Malga Prendera** (2148m). Here AV1 takes n.467, a dirt farm

road via **Forcella Roan** (1999m) – a superb lookout to the majestic Sorapiss and the unmistakable pyramid of the Antelao. A final uphill stretch goes through light wood, and then all of a sudden the Pelmo is incredibly close.

Walkers pause at Forcella Ambrizola

At this range it's easy to understand why **the Pelmo** was dubbed 'Throne of the Gods'. The massive mountain, isolated on all flanks and recognisable from afar for its armchair shape, rises dizzily from scree slopes to 3168m. The first recorded ascent, in 1857, was by British pioneer mountaineer and founder of the Alpine Club, John Ball, but prehistoric hunters probably got there a bit earlier.

At your feet in pretty Val Fiorentina is a typical alpine hut, the well-run **Rifugio Città di Fiume** (1917m, **1hr 30min**).

Rifugio Città di Fiume (tel 0437 720268 or 320 0377432, **www.rifugiocittadifiume.it**, CAI, sleeps

67

The Pelmo looms above Rifugio Città di Fiume

25 in dorms, open mid June to late Sept, credit cards accepted). Don't miss the spicy goulash stew – or the golden sunset on the Pelmo for that matter. Curiously, the hut is the property of the Italian Alpine Club branch once located in Fiume, now known as Rijeka – a port town in Croatia. The border shifted after World War 2, but the name lives on.

Exit (45min)
A farm lane drops to **Malga Fiorentina** for a path heading W to **Rifugio Aquileia** (tel 333 5670303, https://rifugio-aquileia.com) and a camping ground. It's a short way down to the road for the summer bus on the Caprile–Passo Staulanza–Longarone run (Dolomiti Bus).

STAGE 6
Rifugio Città di Fiume to Rifugio Coldai

Start	Rifugio Città di Fiume
Distance	9.3km
Total ascent	560m
Total descent	340m
Grade	2
Time	3hr 30min

After a spectacular opening traverse that gives walkers ample time to appreciate the Pelmo from close quarters, the main AV1 route drops to a road pass. Farms and pasture precede a stiff climb to a wonderful alpine hut in the realms of another awesome stone giant, the Civetta.

However, a choice awaits: an especially rewarding Grade 3 variant on the Sentiero Flaibani embarks on a challenging loop around the Pelmo, taking in the beautifully placed Rifugio Venezia. Climbing to 2476m, this route involves multiple aided stretches. Requirements are the confidence to cover tricky terrain where snow lingers into summer, and not being bothered by heights. Perfect weather is also key as the gullies en route are subject to rockfalls. Much longer than the main AV1, it is best split into two with an overnight stay at either Rifugio Venezia or Palafavera. The two routes meet up at Malga Pioda.

Pelmo variant (6hr)
Leave **Rifugio Città di Fiume** (1917m) on n.480 and branch L on the lane below the buildings. A wide track ascends gently through wood to **Forcella Forada** (1977m). Here, turn sharp R (S) on a narrow path which descends a little. It is not always clear and may be obstructed by springy mountain pines. Soon after traversing a chaotic erosion channel, you reach the strategic steep-sided gully (n.480 on rock). Here Sentiero Flaibani forks L (E) for a tiring clamber that feels near vertical at times.

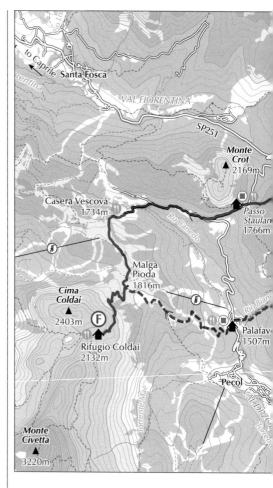

Guided by red paint splashes and occasionally observed by chamois, after a fair slog the path goes L for a section aided by cable and rungs over polished slippery rock. It emerges on a breathtaking crest with a bird's-eye view of the *rifugio* and lots more.

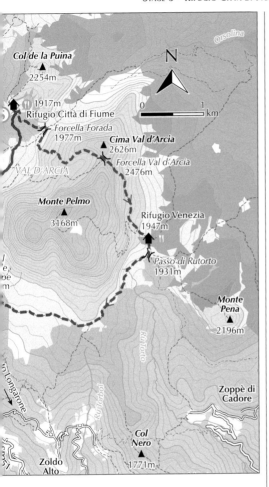

A path leads NE below Cima Forada to gain a grassy ridge frequented by marmots on the northern edge of awesome Val d'Arcia. Keep L through an overwhelming jungle of tumbled rocks and scree, and follow red paint splashes carefully. ▶

Surprisingly bright clumps of Rhaetian poppies flourish in this wilderness.

After hugging a rock face at the base of Cima Val d'Arcia, cross towards the R side of this immense valley and ascend very steeply, finally gaining **Forcella Val d'Arcia** (2476m, **2hr 15min**). It's hard to know which way to look first! Back west is the Marmolada, northwest the terraced Sella massif, while ahead is the unmistakable Antelao triangle, and beyond the spiky Spalti di Toro. ◄

Once you've got your breath back, brace your knees for the descent. The path disappears dramatically over the edge, but take heart as the rubble base is soft and, once you dig your heels in, progression is quite straightforward. Heading ESE, it rounds a rock face guided by fixed cables which come in handy for the narrow passages on crumbly terrain. After a minor saddle the path improves and the *rifugio* comes into sight, as do a multitude of wildflowers. Skirting beneath the Pelmo's prominent Spalla Est (east shoulder), you drop to **Rifugio Venezia** (1947m, **1hr**).

> **Rifugio Venezia** (tel 0436 9684 or 320 0103872, **www.rifugiovenezia.it**, CAI, sleeps 60, open mid June to late Sept). Memorable sunsets, home-made tarts and hearty soups are on the menu. This excellent hut dates back to 1892 and was one of the first in the Dolomites. Used as a base by the partisans during the latter years of World War 2, it was burnt

This dizzy perch is the haunt of perpetually hungry alpine choughs who beg for scraps.

Pelmo variant

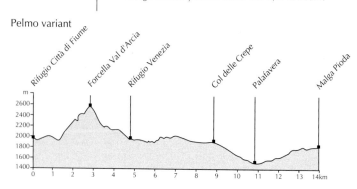

down as a reprisal, but thankfully rebuilt by the
Venice branch of the Alpine Club for re-opening in
1954.

*The final leg up
Val d'Arcia on the
Pelmo variant*

After crossing nearby **Passo di Rutorto** (1931m), AV1
heads decidedly SW on path n.472, dropping across a
rocky basin beneath towering walls. After a subsequent
climb through light wood to a marshy saddle, bear W,
mostly on a level through dwarf mountain pines. At **Col
delle Crepe** (1885m) fork L, following the Rio Bianco
and path n.474 through forest to the road at **Palafavera**
(1507m, **1hr 45min**). Groceries are available at the camping ground, and beds and meals at Rifugio Palafavera. It is
possible to exit the route here (see below).

Rifugio Palafavera (tel 0437 789133, www.
palafavera.it, sleeps 25 in rooms and dorm, open
mid June to mid Sept).

Cross the tarmac for the farm road W up through
forest; several shortcuts are feasible. (The chair lift can
always be used. It terminates at 1889m Col de la Traversa;

73

thereafter is a 10min link path.) The conclusion is former summer farm **Malga Pioda** (1816m, **1hr**) with a fountain and the main AV1 route.

Exit

From Palafavera (see variant above), summer buses (Dolomiti Bus) run down to Forno di Zoldo (tourist info tel 0437 787349, www.valdizoldo.net, shops, ATM, Hotel Mae (tel 0437 788707, www.hotelmae.it)) and on to Longarone for the railway.

Main route

From **Rifugio Città di Fiume** (1917m), at the first bend of the jeep track turn off across a bridge then sharp R on path n.472, descending through light larch wood and heading mostly S. You quickly find yourself on the lower fringe of a yawning scree spread in Val d'Arcia, dwarfed by the Pelmo. Curving SW, cross thickets of low mountain pine before surmounting a minor crest. Keep R at path forks. It's not far down to the road pass and **Rifugio Passo Staulanza** (1766m, **1hr 15min**).

> **Rifugio Passo Staulanza** (tel 338 7900120 or 0437 788709, **www.staulanza.it**, sleeps 50 in rooms and dorm, open early June to late Sept, credit cards accepted). Run by a mountaineer and his family, it makes a pricey stay but promises creature comforts and delicious meals.

Main route

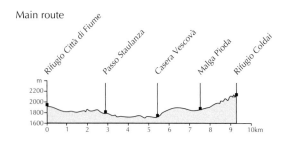

Rifugio Passo Staulanza looks up Val d'Arcia

Exit
A summer Dolomiti Bus runs down Val di Zoldo via villages such as Palafavera (see variant above) and Pecol (tourist info tel 0437 787349, www.valdizoldo.net, ATM, hotels including Hotel Mae, (tel 0437 788707, www.hotelmae.it)) and on to Longarone and the railway.

Head down the road WSW, ignoring turnoffs for Palafavera. At the first bend (1715m) turn R (W) at the colourful cluster of signposts onto n.568, a lane into forest. Further along, keep L to pasture slopes and **Casera Vescovà** (1734m), a dairy farm that excels in meals and refreshments.

Here AV1 forks L off the lane for path n.561, climbing the steep hillside SW. A long, level saddle (1876m)

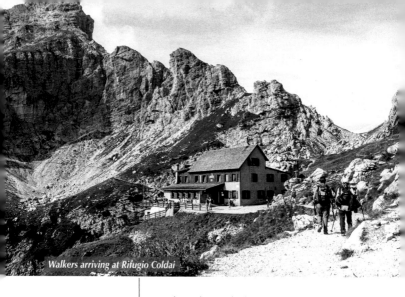
Walkers arriving at Rifugio Coldai

The Pelmo variant slots in at this point.

precedes a dirt road where you go L under Roa Bianca and avalanche barriers. Stick with the road down to former summer farm **Malga Pioda** (1816m, **1hr 15min**) and a drinking water supply. ◄

Very popular with day walkers, n.556/564 starts uphill, the zigzags of the mule track taking the sting from the steepness. The east shoulder of Cima Coldai is gradually rounded as the Civetta is approached. Shortly beyond a goods cableway stands **Rifugio Coldai** (2132m, **1hr**).

Rifugio Coldai (tel 0437 789160, **www.rifugio coldai.com**, CAI, sleeps 83, open mid June to late Sept). A superb hut run by a hospitable local family for the last 50+ years who whip up delicious fruit tarts and wholesome meals for ravenous walkers. A wonderful vantage point for sunsets on the Pelmo, so try and score a seat near the window.

STAGE 7
Rifugio Coldai to Rifugio Vazzoler

Start	Rifugio Coldai
Distance	9.8km
Total ascent	450m
Total descent	850m
Grade	2
Time	3hr 30min

An easy-going and absolutely brilliant stage spent appreciating the phenomenal Civetta, one of the most impressive Dolomite formations. Halfway along the Civetta's lower western wall is lookout par excellence Rifugio Tissi; it's well worth considering an overnight stay here for one of the most spectacular sunsets in the whole of the Dolomites. On the other hand, should you need to leave AV1, a handy 2hr exit route from Rifugio Vazzoler can be followed down to the road at Listolade – see Stage 8.

At **Rifugio Coldai** (2132m), walk along the front terrace then go R, flanking the building. Path n.560 then leads steeply W to gain a rise with a vision of the Marmolada and Sella.

The inviting Lago Coldai

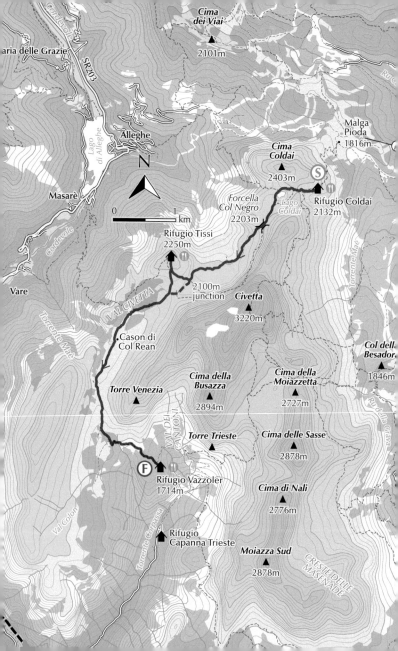

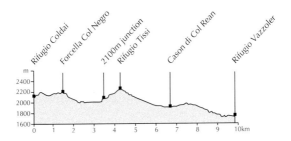

At your feet is the pretty green **Lago Coldai** – a popular picnic spot boasting diminutive beaches, although the temptation to take the plunge should be tempered by the low temperature of the water.

Amid a veritable web of paths, AV1 drops to skirt the R shore of the **lake**, ignoring a turn-off for Alleghe. A climb S via the notch of **Forcella Col Negro** (2203m) is rewarded by your first close-up of the majestic west 'wall of walls'. ▶

Despite the chaotic scree, mountain avens and yellow poppies flourish.

Shaped like an enormous trident and likened to a set of organ pipes, the **Civetta** rises majestically between the deep-cut Cordevole river valley and smiling pastures of Val Zoldana. Soaring to 3220m, it was first scaled in 1867 by British mountaineer Francis Fox Tuckett. The slender rock barrier extends north–south for 6km, its southern extremity linked to the Moiazza, as will be seen in Stage 8.

AV1 loses a fair bit of height on the ensuing tiring descent with loose stones. Ricocheting rock discharges resound of an afternoon, so stick to the safe main route and don't be tempted by higher shortcuts – most disappear in any case, obliterated by debris, obliging walkers into awkward dangerous clambering. Good news are the bird's-eye views to Alleghe and its green lake, formed in the 1700s after a mammoth landslip from a polished oblique slab, clearly visible.

More ups and downs await, and another fork to Alleghe is passed. An uphill leg finally reaches the well-marked **2100m junction** for Rifugio Tissi. Only if time is tight (a saving of 30min) should this section be missed. (The direct route continues SW to where the main route joins in Val Civetta).

Fork R (NW) for the steep slog up to the marvellous rock perch of cheerful **Rifugio Tissi** (2250m, **1hr 45min**).

> **Rifugio Tissi** (tel 0437 721644, **www.rifugiotissi. com**, CAI, sleeps 70, open mid June to late Sept). Although the water may not be suitable for drinking here, the beer certainly is, and is best enjoyed from the panoramic terrace. For dinner, don't miss the delicious *pasta al ragù*. Towards evening the hut empties as the sun goes down and everyone heads up the hill (Cima di Col Rean) marked by a crucifix, to drink in the divine technicolour show the Civetta puts on.

Waiting for sunset on the Civetta near Rifugio Tissi

Rifugio Vazzoler welcomes walkers at the stage end

Resume the AV1 without returning to the 2100m junction: instead retrace your steps a short way downhill to where the clear n.560 branches R, heading S to **Val Civetta**. Soon there's soft grassy terrain – a comfort for the feet after all that scree, although watch out for mud. The vegetation picks up too with larch, juniper and pink spreads of alpenrose, and a pasture plain with the derelict **Cason di Col Rean**.

Further along, gigantic stone cubes lie in the shadow of soaring Torre Venezia, the Civetta's easternmost trident point. As the path rounds this southernmost corner, the fairytale turrets and spires of the Moiazza appear through the trees, topped by Moiazza Nord. At a gravelly farm road turn L (ESE) for the brief stroll to the beautiful conifer wood where welcoming **Rifugio Vazzoler** (1714m, **1hr 45min**) is ensconced.

Rifugio Vazzoler (tel 0437 660008 or 340 1612828, **www.rifugiovazzoler.com**, CAI, sleeps 80, open mid June to late Sept). This relaxed rambling *rifugio* stands at the base of Val dei Cantoni with the twin rock bastions Torre Venezia and Torre Trieste guarding their respective corners. Inside the hut, a model of the Civetta aids in understanding the layout of the giant. Outside, a lovely botanical garden boasts alpine flower specimens both common and rare.

STAGE 8
Rifugio Vazzoler to Rifugio Carestiato

Start	Rifugio Vazzoler
Distance	8.7km
Total ascent	620m
Total descent	500m
Grade	2+
Time	3hr 20min

At lower altitudes than previous stages but no less beautiful, today you progress beneath a breathtaking line-up of soaring rock walls and towers belonging to the Siamese-twinned Civetta and Moiazza groups. Clear paths with the odd tricky stretch follow a fine line between vast conifer forests and scree slopes. In view of the relative brevity of this stage and its manageable height gain and loss, it can feasibly be extended to Passo Duran (Stage 9) for more accommodation options.

A handy exit route from Rifugio Vazzoler drops to a road and public transport at Listolade.

Exit route to Listolade (2hr)
The jeep track (n.555) that serves **Rifugio Vazzoler** can be followed in descent all the way S to Val Corpassa and a car park near **Rifugio Capanna Trieste** (1135m, 1hr 10min).

Rifugio Capanna Trieste (tel 0437 660122 or 340 5028699, www.rifugiocapannatrieste.it, sleeps 18, open May to Oct). The homely café-eatery specialises in divine gnocchi with smoked ricotta. If desired, a taxi can be booked for pick-up here to Listolade, Alleghe and elsewhere (tel 348 5658675 Agordo taxi, or tel 340 6796016 www.taxialleghe.com).

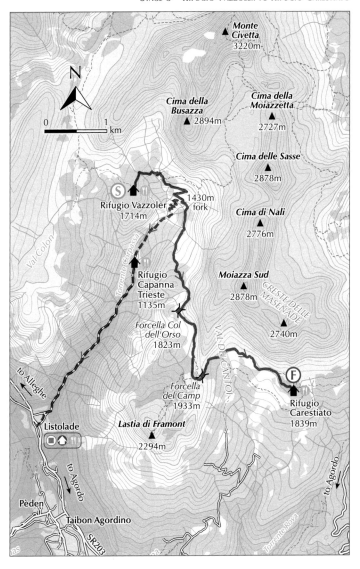

A narrow surfaced road continues 4km down to **Listolade** (701m, **50min**) for bustling bar/restaurant/hotel Albergo Monte Civetta (tel 0437 660050) and year-round buses (Dolomiti Bus) to Belluno or Alleghe.

Main route

In the opposite direction to the Civetta, across Val Cordevole, elegant Monte Agner appears, its lofty point floating above the tiny settlement of Listolade.

Leave **Rifugio Vazzoler** (1714m) on the gravelled jeep track n.555 that curves NE at first through conifer cover across the bottom of Val dei Cantoni, affording more magnificent views of the Civetta's fantastic towers. ◄ Ignore the turn-off for Rifugio Torrani and continue a good way downhill to the key **fork** (1430m, **30min**) where AV1 leaves the jeep track to head L (S) into beautiful wood on n.554.

Accompanied by squirrels and masses of wildflowers, the path crosses a stream beneath Spiz della Mussaia then embarks on a steady climb through beech wood. Eroded gullies are crossed as the amazing west wall of the Moiazza is approached. A steep and exposed but short clamber brings you to **Forcella Col dell'Orso** (1823m, **1hr 15min**), a reminder of the bears that once roamed these mountains (*orso* means 'bear'). A pause here is in order to take in the inspiring sights of the Pale di San Martino Altipiano to the south, and closer at hand more Moiazza wonders.

The rock faces feature an astounding range of precious blooms such as devil's claw and endemic bellflowers.

Through springy dwarf pines, AV1 turns S across the head of wild, isolated Busa del Camp. A brief cable-aided passage helps you around an outcrop before a little more uphill sees you navigating boulders. ◄

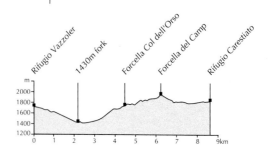

Where the path forks, ignore arrows L and keep straight on to a pasture valley. A junction near the ruins of Casera del Camp precedes a short climb to red-clay **Forcella del Camp** (1933m, **45min**) and the breathtaking spectacle of the Moiazza Sud with its countless spires. Luckily, a matter of minutes down the other side, a bench at a crucifix lets you appreciate the line-up in comfort.

Not far downhill, you traverse E through larch wood alive with twittering finches and views to the destination *rifugio* on its wooded promontory, backed by another vision – the San Sebastiano-Tamer range, where AV1 ventures during the next stage. You proceed across Val dei Cantoi and will inevitably be joined by climbers returning from the renowned Ferrata Costantini, one of the longest and most difficult via ferratas in the whole of the Dolomites. A final jaunt across scree and through woodland leads to bright and modern **Rifugio Carestiato** (1839m, **1hr 35min**).

On the way to
Forcella del Camp

Rifugio Carestiato (tel 0437 62949, **www. rifugiocarestiato.com**, CAI, sleeps 57 in shared rooms, open late June to late Sept, credit cards accepted, laundry facilities).

STAGE 9

Rifugio Carestiato to Rifugio Pramperet

Start	Rifugio Carestiato
Distance	13.2km
Total ascent	620m
Total descent	600m
Grade	2
Time	4hr 20min

A divine day's walking. It begins by tracing the base of the awesome eastern Moiazza before reaching a road pass with refreshments, meals and accommodation. AV1 then enters the realms of the Parco Nazionale delle Dolomiti Bellunesi, heading through beautiful woodland and quieter, less frequented places dominated by the spectacular San Sebastiano-Tamer mountains. A friendly albeit simple *rifugio*, one of the few manned huts in this wild park, awaits at day's end.

From **Rifugio Carestiato** (1839m) a clear white gravel lane is followed E across pasture clearings and light wood. A path shortcuts the last leg down to the road at **Passo Duran** (1601m, **40min**), at the foot of the impressive Cima Nord di San Sebastiano. There are no bus services but there are two good refreshment/meal places and overnight options.

> **Rifugio Passo Duran** aka Rifugio C. Tomè (tel 346 4165461, www.rifugiopassoduran.it, sleeps 22 in rooms and dorm, open mid June to late Sept, credit cards accepted, laundry facilities). Offering reasonable rates and generous buffet breakfast, this *rifugio* is run by the family of an alpine guide.
>
> **Rifugio San Sebastiano** (tel 0437 62360, www.passoduran.it, sleeps 25 in rooms, open

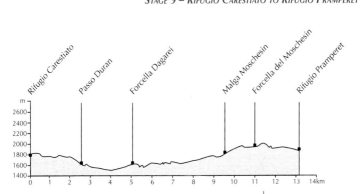

year-round, credit cards accepted). Hotel-style accommodation. Dinner options include home-made soups and hearty meat stews served around an open fireplace. The owner has a wonderful collection of fossils – check out the ammonites and megalodont shells.

AV1 proceeds downhill R (S) on the surfaced road for 2km, ignoring a turn-off for Malga Caleda. The open outlook takes in the Vette Feltrine and the glacier-smoothed Pale di San Martino. Where the road veers W to cross a stream, take the fork (1493m, **20min**) with picnic tables, where AV1/n.543 breaks off L (SW) into the realms of Parco Nazionale delle Dolomiti Bellunesi. High above is the yawning gully Van de Caleda separating San Sebastiano from the Tamer massif which now dominates the way.

The going (S) gets steep as you enter cool conifer forest, which is soft underfoot, and you gain **Forcella Dagarei** (1620m). Not far after an old hut, the path emerges onto blinding white scree colonised by dwarf mountain pines, skirting the Tamer towers and chaotic rockfalls. ▸

The panorama is vast, even taking in the Cordevole valley and its villages.

AV1 proceeds effortlessly below Cima delle Forzelete before curving S, dominated by the imposing Castello di Moschesin. Woodland of larch and pine shades walkers on the climb to the lovely picnic spot

87

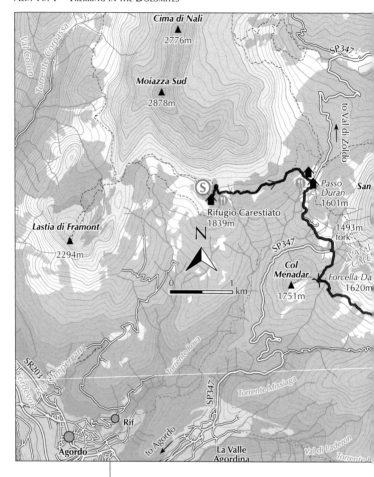

Casera or **Malga Moschesin** (1800m, drinking water, emergency shelter). A short climb E concludes at a brilliant lookout at 1966m – ahead now are the Cime de Zita and Talvena.

Coasting along the top of Val Clusa, the path reaches abandoned barracks at the ample saddle of **Forcella del**

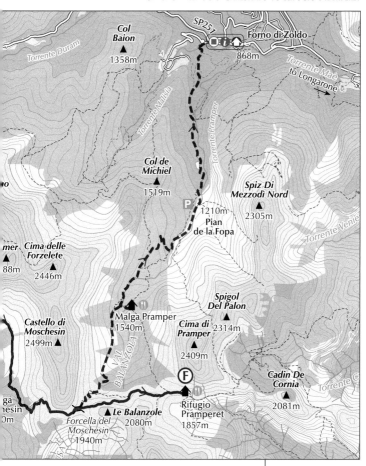

Moschesin (1940m, **2hr 30min**) in a veritable sea of mountain pines, alpenrose and bellflowers. ▸

Exit to Forno di Zoldo (2hr 45min)
If needs be, take path n.540 in descent N via **Val Balanzola**. The modernised working summer dairy

The surrounding rocky realms conceal shy chamois, as well as wartime shelters and tunnel systems.

89

farm **Malga Pramper** (1540m, **45min**) offers delicious home-made cakes, meals and a dorm for eight (tel 329 7862899). From here a jeep shuttle (tel 348 6700786, weekends Jul + Sept, daily Aug or on request) runs via Pian de la Fopa (1210m) to Forno di Zoldo (868m). Otherwise allow 2hr on foot all the way. Forno: tourist info tel 0437 787349, www.valdizoldo.net; hotels, ATM, shops, Dolomiti Bus to Longarone for trains.

Main route

Ignore the path for Malga Pramper and keep R for a modest rise (1980m) with magnificent views north to the Zoldo valley backed by the Pelmo, Sorapiss and Antelao. ◀ Heading E, descend a little to round **Le Balanzole** and drop to join a lower path. A final short climb leads past the junction needed in Stage 10, as you stroll towards the **hut** (1857m, **50min**), which only appears at the last minute as it is surrounded by trees.

Ahead to the northeast is the isolated Cima di Pramper.

Rifugio Pramperet aka Sommariva (tel 0437 1956153, **www.rifugiosommarivaalpramperet.it**, CAI, sleeps 25 in dorms, open mid June to late Sept). Originally a simple hut used by hunters, it now offers basic facilities and tasty meals in a peaceful setting.

Rifugio Pramperet is a popular place

STAGE 10

Rifugio Pramperet to Rifugio Pian de Fontana

Start	Rifugio Pramperet
Distance	6.2km
Total ascent	540m
Total descent	760m
Grade	2–3
Time	3hr

One of the best stages on the whole of AV1, this deserves to be taken slowly in order to drink in the magnificent rugged scenery of the Dolomiti Bellunesi. Quiet and wild, far from civilisation, with wildlife sightings pretty well guaranteed. Slopes are carpeted with superb wildflowers; many are survivors from ice age 'islands' which harboured seeds from warmer climes. Examples are dwarf broom and mountain tragacanth, a type of milk vetch. The surrounds of Monte Talvena are a special reserve and walkers should not stray from marked paths.

In terms of difficulty, there's a short clamber up a moderately exposed ridge during the ascent. Further on, the final descent to Rifugio Pian de Fontana is pretty steep, and extra care is recommended.

If you have energy to burn you may prefer to extend the stage to Rifugio Bianchet – but be aware that it's a further 2hr 15min (Stage 11).

From **Rifugio Pramperet** (1857m) retrace your steps to the junction passed in Stage 9, and branch L (SW) on path n.514. A gentle climb ensues, the mountain pine vegetation giving way to thrift and saxifrage as things get stonier. A saddle – **Portela del Piazedel** (2097m) – is the first of today's many lookout spots, this one taking in Castello di Moschesin and beyond to the Moiazza. However, things improve fantastically as you proceed steadily S across inclined limestone slabs amid rock jasmine and bevies of Rhaetian poppies. A final steep slog leads to a narrow,

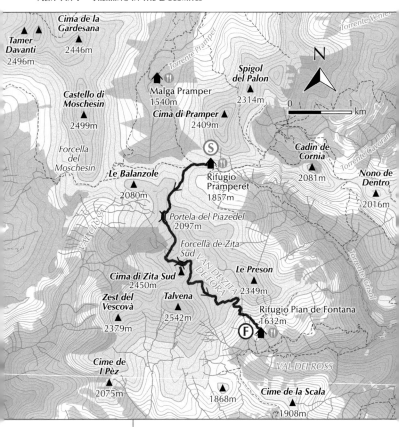

Around are immense stratified formations, notably Talvena, due south.

exciting ridge (2351m), whose flanks plunge crazily to Val de Erbandoi. ◄

Now for the steep but short hands-on ascent E up a near-vertical crest with a little exposure. You quickly gain broader grassy terraces where there is more space to admire the stunning views to Castello di Moschesin and, beyond, the spread of the Moiazza.

It's not far at all to **Forcella de Zita Sud** (2395m, **1hr 40min**), the gateway to a beautiful valley: Van de Zita de

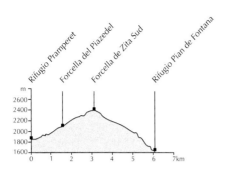

Fora, scooped out by ancient glaciers and home to herds of chamois and colonies of romping marmots whose burrows pit the mountainsides. In the meantime, close at hand is a highly recommended detour.

Cima di Zita Sud (15min return)
Cairns mark the start of a faint path that heads R (S) up the inclined slab to **Cima di Zita Sud** (2450m) and wide-reaching views. Retrace your steps to the main route.

Walkers descending the vast slab incline of Cima di Zita Sud

It's a gentle descent on alternating grass and grey scree slopes brightened by pink thrift blooms. All around are vast horizontal limestone tiers run through with grooves and rut channelling, the outcome of widespread karstification. Veering S, you drop between the craggy Cima di Zita Sud and a prominent ridge that culminates in Le Preson. ◄

The landscape is lunar, and the frequent dolina hollows harbour wildflowers.

At the 2000m mark the path narrows and goes over a pronounced lip; a sign warns it is steep ahead. You traverse E, hugging rock faces studded with edelweiss and saxifrage. To the south the marvellous vision of the twin Schiara and Pelf is revealed, with the curious rock spike of Gusela del Vescovà ('bishop's needle') – said to have provided anchorage for Noah's Ark, no less!

The *rifugio* comes into view but it's still a fair way down. The going (SE) becomes especially steep with loose stones underfoot – take extra care not to lose your footing. The last section to **Rifugio Pian de Fontana** (1632m, **1hr 20min**) is flanked by a bright red outcrop, which explains the valley name: Val dei Ross.

> **Rifugio Pian de Fontana** (tel 335 6096819 or 0437 1956135, **www.piandefontana.it**, CAI, sleeps 33 in dorms, open early June to late Sept). A clutch of nicely converted shepherds' huts, one of which serves as a cosy dining room with a roaring fire – the perfect setting for a dinner of mounds of steaming polenta smothered with melted local cheese or *pastin* (a local sausage). The hut's open setting makes it a good spot for observing birds of prey.

STAGE 11

Rifugio Pian de Fontana to La Pissa bus stop

Start	Rifugio Pian de Fontana
Distance	11km
Total ascent	200m
Total descent	1400m
Grade	2
Time	4hr 15min

This wonderful conclusion to AV1 crosses into wild Val Vescovà (bishop's valley), dominated by the giant Schiara, which rises to a giddy 2565m. The mountain name is believed to derive from the Celtic for 'rings', once used as boundary markers here. A fascinating story narrates that Saint Martin came this way and tied his horse to one of these rings, which turned into pure gold!

Near its foot is the well-run Rifugio Bianchet, a fine place to lunch if not stay the night to relax and delay the return to 'civilisation'. Afterwards you descend a dramatic ravine in beautiful, rugged surrounds on a well-graded track, straightforward if long – there's 1400m height loss in all for this stage. The conclusion is at roadside La Pissa in Val Cordevole for the bus to Belluno.

BUSES FROM LA PISSA

Timetables and tickets for Dolomiti Bus are available at Rifugio Bianchet – it's a good idea to buy tickets here to save holding up the bus when you board (the driver will definitely appreciate it), and this way you avoid paying the modest onboard surcharge. A final hint is to try to time your arrival at La Pissa to coincide with a bus as there's no shelter or anywhere nice to wait.

From **Rifugio Pian de Fontana** (1632m), n.514 takes you SSW through beautiful beech wood, quickly losing height. At a stream (1490m), AV1 forks R for a testing, zigzagging climb out of Val dei Ross and across the foot of an awesome amphitheatre.

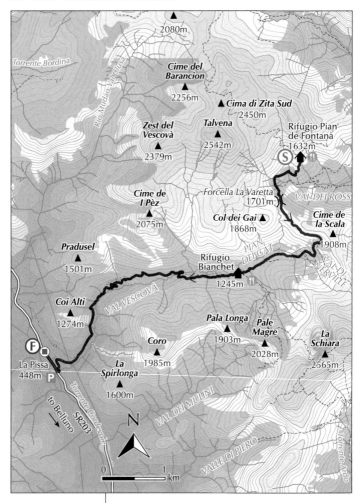

After more woodland you gain ample **Forcella La Varetta** (1701m, **1hr**). The Schiara rears up majestically at surprisingly close quarters now, hugely dominant, across thickly wooded Val Vescovà. You turn SE on an old

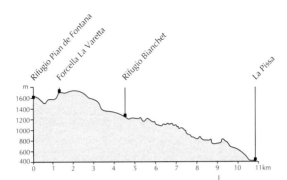

herder's trail, a narrow but beautiful path cutting below Cime de la Scala. ▶

The path finally begins to drop, mostly SW, ignoring a fork for a via ferrata. Continue down the Scalon (big staircase) to where tired feet will appreciate the soft leaf litter in the beech wood. Once you reach the valley floor the gradient eases and it's not far through conifer forest to the divine clearing of **Pian dei Gat** with thrilling Schiara views and the spacious **Rifugio Bianchet** (1245m, **1hr 15min**).

The rock flanks here are a veritable alpine botanical garden with myriad saxifrage and edelweiss to name but two.

Welcoming Rifugio Bianchet occupies a lovely spot

The magnificent Schiara with the Gusela rock needle dominate this stage

It's amazing to think that local shepherds herded their flocks up this forbidding valley to the high pastures until the 1960s.

Rifugio Bianchet (tel 0437 669226 or 335 6446975, rifugiobianchet@hotmail.com, CAI, sleeps 40 in comfortable rooms and dorm, open beg June to end Sept).

A good gravel lane for supplying the hut leads gently downhill W, crossing a bridge to the R side of Val Vescovà. A rapid series of hairpin bends and occasional shortcuts come next. Thick woods of conifer and beech flourish below towering cliffs that close in as you proceed. ◄ Ahead, the wild Monti del Sole appear above the treetops.

As the ravine opens a little, about an hour and a half from Rifugio Bianchet, AV1/n.503 leaves the lane, breaking off as a path L (signed *Fermata autobus* – bus stop). Narrow and steep in spots, it can be slippery due to exposed tree roots. The Val Cordevole floor finally comes into view below, and before you know it you're down at a footbridge over a gaping chasm complete with a cascade and pool.

Steps lead to the roadside at **La Pissa** (448m, **2hr**). Turn R past a car park and walk along the road for 400 metres. The **bus stop** for Belluno is on the opposite side of the road near a derelict house.

LEAVING THE ROUTE

It's a 20min trip to the pleasant alpine town of Belluno (370m), whose name is derived from the Celtic for 'splendid hill' – its backdrop is the sheer south face of the Schiara. Well served with shops, ATMs, cafés, restaurants and a hospital, it is a good transport hub with rail services south to Venice as well as trains north to Calalzo for ongoing buses to Cortina.

But before you leave, drop in to the Belluno tourist office (Piazza Duomo 2, tel 334 2813222, http://adorable.belluno.it). On presentation of the *rifugi* stamps you've collected en route, you'll be congratulated and rewarded with a well-earned Alta Via 1 badge.

Should you decide to stay over here, accommodation options include centrally located Albergo delle Alpi (tel 0437 940545, www.dellealpi.it) and B&B La Cerva (tel 338 8253608, www.lacerva.it/it/).

VIA FERRATA

AV1 traditionally concluded with the Via Ferrata Marmol over the Schiara to Rifugio 7° Alpini, then on to Belluno. This has not been described here as it is a difficult aided climbing route, not a walk. Moreover, walkers intending to embark on the VF need to lug the gear with them for days on end, as it is only needed for the route conclusion. However, should the Via Ferrata Marmol appeal to you, by all means book the services of a qualified alpine guide who can also supply the necessary equipment. Contact Marino De Colle at www.wildmountain.it tel 349 8201331.

This route means 7/8 hours from Rifugio Pian de Fontana to Rifugio 7° Alpini (1502m). The following day means descent to Case Bortot (694m, 2hr). A minor road leads 3km down to the main road at Bolzano Bellunese (541m, 45min) for Dolomiti Bus the rest of the way to Belluno.

APPENDIX A
Useful contacts

Tourist information

Italian Tourist Board
The Italian Tourist Board, ENIT (www.enit.it), has offices all over the world and inspiring websites crammed with all manner of helpful info for intending travellers.

UK (London office)
tel 020 74081254
www.italia.it

Australia (Sydney office)
tel 02 93572561
https://visitaly.com.au

USA (New York office)
tel (212) 2455618
www.italiantourism.com

Local tourist offices useful for Alta Via 1
Agordo
tel 0437 62105
www.agordo.net

Arabba
tel 0436 79130
www.arabba.it

Belluno
tel 334 2813222
www.adorablebelluno.it

Braies
tel 0474 748660
https://www.prags.bz/en

Cortina d'Ampezzo
tel 0436 869086
www.dolomiti.org

Dobbiaco
tel 0474 972132
www.dobbiaco.bz

Pecol, Val di Zoldo
tel 0437789145
www.valdizoldo.net/it/info/uffici-turistici-zoldo

Villabassa
tel 0474 745136
www.tre-cime.info/it/villabassa.html

Parks on Alta Via 1
Parco Naturale Fanes-Senes-Braies
https://nature-parks.provinz.bz.it

Parco Naturale delle Dolomiti d'Ampezzo
www.dolomitiparco.com

Parco Nazionale delle Dolomiti Bellunesi
www.dolomitipark.it

Transport

Trains
Eurostar
www.eurostar.com

France
www.sncf.com

Germany
www.bahn.com

Italy
www.trenitalia.com

Buses
ATVO
www.atvo.it

Cortina Express
www.cortinaexpress.it

Dolomiti Bus
https://dolomitibus.it

SAD
www.sad.it

Airports
Venice
www.veniceairport.com

Treviso
www.trevisoairport.it

Private transfers
www.transferdolomiti.it

www.dolomititransfer.net

www.claudiobus.eu

www.taxialleghe.com

Weather
Südtirol
https://weather.provinz.bz.it

Trentino
www.meteotrentino.it

Veneto
www.arpa.veneto.it

Emergencies
General emergency
tel 112

Soccorso alpino (mountain rescue)
tel 118

APPENDIX B
Italian–English glossary

Italian	English
acqua (non) potabile	water (not) suitable for drinking
agriturismo	farm with meals and/or accommodation
aiuto!	help!
albergo	hotel
alimentari	grocery shop
alpe	mountain pasture
alto	high
altopiano, altipiano	high altitude plateau, upland
aperto	open
autostazione	bus station
bagno	bathroom or toilet
baita	alpine shepherd's hut, sometimes a farm or refuge
basso	low
bivacco	bivouac hut, unmanned
bosco	wood
burrone	ravine
bus, busa	cirque
cabinovia	gondola car lift
caduta sassi	rock falls
campanile	rock spire (bell tower)
campeggio	camping, camping ground

Italian	English
capanna	hut
carta escursionistica	walking map
cascata	waterfall
casera	hut
caserma	barracks
cengia	ledge
chiuso	closed
cima	mountain peak
col	hill, mountain or saddle
croce	cross
croda	mountain peak
cuccetta	bunk bed
custode	hut guardian
destra	right
difficile	difficult
diga	dam
discesa	descent
doccia fredda/calda	cold/hot shower
est	east
facile	easy
fermata dell'autobus	bus stop
fiume	river
fontana	fountain

Italian	English
forcella	saddle, pass
funivia	cable-car
galleria	tunnel
gettone	token (for a shower in the rifugi)
ghiacciaio	glacier
giro	tour
grande	large
grotta	cave
lago	lake
malga	mountain farm, sometimes a refuge
meridione	south
meteo	weather forecast
mezzo	middle
molino, mulino	mill
monte	mountain
nevaio	snow field
nord	north
nuovo percorso	new routing
occidente	west
ometto	cairn (little man)
orario	timetable
oriente	east
orrido	ravine
ovest	west
panificio	bakery
passo	pass, saddle

Italian	English
percorso alpinistico/ attrezzato	climbing/aided route
pericolo	danger
pian	level ground
piccolo	small
ponte	bridge
previsioni del tempo	weather forecast
pronto soccorso	first aid, hospital emergency department
punta	mountain peak
rifugio	manned mountain hut
rio	mountain stream
salita	ascent
scorciatoia	shortcut
seggiovia	chair lift
sella	saddle, pass
sentiero	path
settentrione	north
sinistra	left
soccorso alpino	mountain rescue
sorgente	spring (water)
spiz	mountain peak
stazione ferroviaria	railway station
strada	road
sud	south

Italian	English
tappa	stage
telecabina	gondola car lift
teleferica	aerial goods cableway
torre	tower
torrente	mountain stream
val, valle, vallone	valley

Italian	English
van	cirque
vetta	mountain peak
via ferrata	aided climbing route
via normale	climbing route
vietato!	forbidden!

NOTES

NOTES

NOTES

DOWNLOAD THE ROUTES
IN GPX FORMAT

All the routes in this guide are available for download from:

www.cicerone.co.uk/1081/GPX

as standard format GPX files. You should be able to load them into most online GPX systems and mobile devices, whether GPS or smartphone. You may need to convert the file into your preferred format using a conversion programme such as gpsvisualizer.com or one of the many other such websites and programmes.

When you follow this link, you will be asked for your email address and where you purchased the guidebook, and have the option to subscribe to the Cicerone e-newsletter.

www.cicerone.co.uk

LISTING OF CICERONE GUIDES

BRITISH ISLES CHALLENGES, COLLECTIONS AND ACTIVITIES

Cycling Land's End to John o' Groats
Great Walks on the England Coast Path
The Big Rounds
The Book of the Bivvy
The Book of the Bothy
The Mountains of England & Wales:
Vol 1 Wales
Vol 2 England
The National Trails
Walking the End to End Trail

SCOTLAND

Ben Nevis and Glen Coe
Cycle Touring in Northern Scotland
Cycling in the Hebrides
Great Mountain Days in Scotland
Mountain Biking in Southern and Central Scotland
Mountain Biking in West and North West Scotland
Not the West Highland Way
Scotland
Scotland's Mountain Ridges
Scottish Wild Country Backpacking
Skye's Cuillin Ridge Traverse
The Borders Abbeys Way
The Great Glen Way
The Great Glen Way Map Booklet
The Hebridean Way
The Hebrides
The Isle of Mull
The Isle of Skye
The Skye Trail
The Southern Upland Way
The Speyside Way
The Speyside Way Map Booklet
The West Highland Way
The West Highland Way Map Booklet
Walking Ben Lawers, Rannoch and Atholl
Walking in the Cairngorms
Walking in the Pentland Hills
Walking in the Scottish Borders
Walking in the Southern Uplands
Walking in Torridon, Fisherfield, Fannichs and An Teallach
Walking Loch Lomond and the Trossachs
Walking on Arran
Walking on Harris and Lewis
Walking on Jura, Islay and Colonsay
Walking on Rum and the Small Isles
Walking on the Orkney and Shetland Isles
Walking on Uist and Barra

Walking the Cape Wrath Trail
Walking the Corbetts
Vol 1 South of the Great Glen
Vol 2 North of the Great Glen
Walking the Galloway Hills
Walking the John o' Groats Trail
Walking the Munros
Vol 1 – Southern, Central and Western Highlands
Vol 2 – Northern Highlands and the Cairngorms
Winter Climbs: Ben Nevis and Glen Coe

NORTHERN ENGLAND ROUTES

Cycling the Reivers Route
Cycling the Way of the Roses
Hadrian's Cycleway
Hadrian's Wall Path
Hadrian's Wall Path Map Booklet
Short Walks Hadrian's Wall
The Coast to Coast Cycle Route
The Coast to Coast Walk
The Coast to Coast Map Booklet
The Pennine Way
The Pennine Way Map Booklet
Walking the Dales Way
Walking the Dales Way Map Booklet

NORTH-EAST ENGLAND, YORKSHIRE DALES AND PENNINES

Cycling in the Yorkshire Dales
Great Mountain Days in the Pennines
Mountain Biking in the Yorkshire Dales
St Oswald's Way and St Cuthbert's Way
The Cleveland Way and the Yorkshire Wolds Way
The Cleveland Way Map Booklet
The North York Moors
The Reivers Way
Trail and Fell Running in the Yorkshire Dales
Walking in County Durham
Walking in Northumberland
Walking in the North Pennines
Walking in the Yorkshire Dales: North and East
South and West

NORTH-WEST ENGLAND AND THE ISLE OF MAN

Cycling the Pennine Bridleway
Isle of Man Coastal Path
Short Walks in Arnside and Silverdale
The Lancashire Cycleway
The Lune Valley and Howgills

Walking in Cumbria's Eden Valley
Walking in Lancashire
Walking in the Forest of Bowland and Pendle
Walking on the Isle of Man
Walking on the West Pennine Moors
Walks in Silverdale and Arnside

LAKE DISTRICT

Cycling in the Lake District
Great Mountain Days in the Lake District
Joss Naylor's Lakes, Meres and Waters of the Lake District
Lake District Winter Climbs
Lake District: High Level and Fell Walks
Lake District: Low Level and Lake Walks
Mountain Biking in the Lake District
Outdoor Adventures with Children – Lake District
Scrambles in the Lake District – North
Scrambles in the Lake District – South
Short Walks in the Lake District: Windermere Ambleside and Grasmere
Trail and Fell Running in the Lake District
Walking The Cumbria Way
Walking the Lake District Fells:
Borrowdale
Buttermere
Coniston
Keswick
Langdale
Mardale and the Far East
Patterdale
Wasdale
Walking the Tour of the Lake District

DERBYSHIRE, PEAK DISTRICT AND MIDLANDS

Cycling in the Peak District
Dark Peak Walks
Scrambles in the Dark Peak
Walking in Derbyshire
Walking in the Peak District – White Peak East
Walking in the Peak District – White Peak West

SOUTHERN ENGLAND

20 Classic Sportive Rides in South East England
20 Classic Sportive Rides in South West England
Cycling in the Cotswolds

For full information on all our guides, books and eBooks, visit our website:
www.cicerone.co.uk

CICERONE

Trust Cicerone to guide your next adventure,
wherever it may be around the world...

Discover guides for hiking, mountain walking, backpacking,
trekking, trail running, cycling and mountain biking, ski touring,
climbing and scrambling in Britain, Europe and worldwide.

Connect with Cicerone online and find inspiration.

- buy books and ebooks
- articles, advice and trip reports
- podcasts and live events
- GPX files and updates
- regular newsletter

cicerone.co.uk